COPPER LODGE LIBRARY

SELF-RELIANCE
AND ESSAYS ON THE NATURE OF MAN

RALPH WALDO EMERSON

ANNOTATED BY
Stephanie Bailey Meter

MULTIMEDIA

Self-Reliance and Essays on the Nature of Man (Copper Lodge Library)

© 2019 Classical Conversations® MultiMedia. All rights reserved.

Published by Classical Conversations, Inc.
255 Air Tool Drive
Southern Pines, NC 28387

CLASSICALCONVERSATIONS.COM
CLASSICALCONVERSATIONSBOOKS.COM

Cover design by Classical Conversations.

The cover artwork and colored illustrations were collected from a variety of illustrators.

Printed in the United States of America

All rights reserved. No part of this publication may be reproduced, stored in a retrieval system, or transmitted in any form by any means, electronic, mechanical, photocopy, recording, or otherwise, without prior permission of the author, except as provided by USA copyright law.

ISBN: 978-1-7329639-9-3

TABLE OF CONTENTS

Self-Reliance	7
Shakspeare; or, the Poet	43
Thoreau	71
Courage	99
Success	123

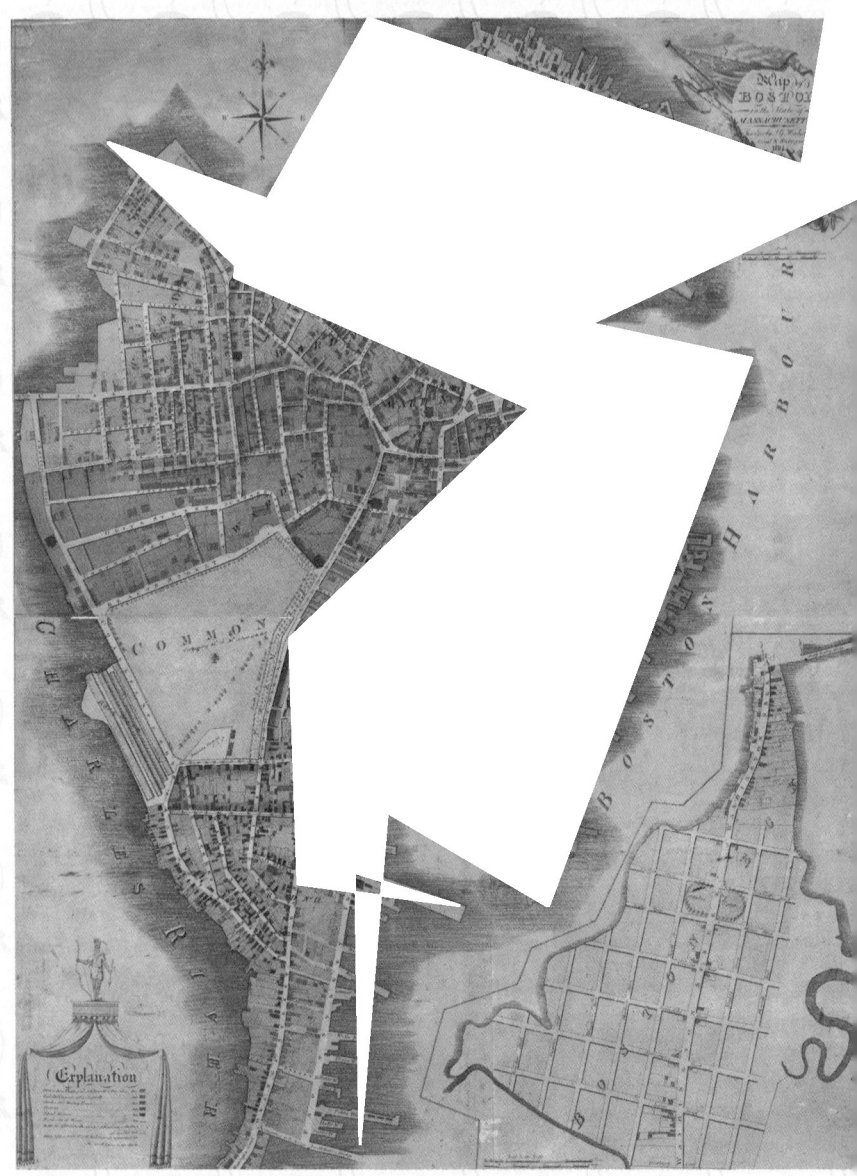

BOSTON, MASSACHUSETTS of 1814.

- **1803** *born* in Boston. Father dies when he is 8; raised by his mother and an aunt.
- **1812** *attends* Boston Latin School.
- **1817** *enrolls* Harvard College, Cambridge. Class Poet.
- **1821–1825** *teaches* at his brother's school.
- **1824–1828** *attends* Harvard Divinity School.
- **1829** *marries* Ellen Louisa Tucker (1811–1831).

ABOVE: Harvard Gate at Harvard University, 1899.

AT LEFT: Emerson, engraving by Stephen A. Schoff from an original drawing by Sam W. Rowse, 1878.

- **1833** *travels* to Europe.
- **1833** *begins* a lecture career that lasts almost fifty years.
- **1834** *returns* to Cambridge to live with his step-grandfather at the Old Manse.
- **1835** *marries* Lydia [Lidian] Jackson. They move to Emerson House.
- **1837** *meets* Henry David Thoreau.
- **1841** *publishes* "Self-Reliance" in *Essays*.

The Unitarian Church from *Old Concord* by Allen French (1870–1946) and Lester G. Hornby, published in 1915.

SELF-RELIANCE

"Ne te quæsiveris extra."[1]
—*Persius, Sat. I. 7. Compare Macrobius, Com. in Somn. Scip., I. ix. 3, and Boethius, De Consol. Phil., IV. 4*

"Man is his own star; and the soul that can
Render an honest and a perfect man,
Commands all light, all influence, all fate;
Nothing to him falls early or too late.
Our acts our angels are, or good or ill,
Our fatal shadows that walk by us still."
—Epilogue to Beaumont and Fletcher's *Honest Man's Fortune*

Cast the bantling[2] on the rocks,
Suckle him with the she-wolf's teat;
Wintered with the hawk and fox,
Power and speed be hands and feet.
—"Power" from *Quatrains* (Emerson)

---

1. Latin: "Do not seek anything outside of yourself."
2. Pronounced BAN't-leeng. A child.

1 I read the other day some verses written by an eminent[1] painter which were original and not conventional. The soul always hears an admonition[2] in such lines, let the subject be what it may. The sentiment they instill is of more value than any thought they may contain. To believe your own thought, to believe that what is true for you in your private heart is true for all men,—that is genius. Speak your latent[3] conviction, and it shall be the universal sense; for the inmost in due time becomes the outmost,—and our first thought is rendered back to us by the trumpets of the Last Judgment. Familiar as the voice of the mind is to each, the highest merit we ascribe to Moses, Plato,[4] and Milton[5] is, that they set at naught books and traditions, and spoke not what men, but what they thought. A man should learn to detect and watch that gleam of light which flashes across his mind from within, more than the luster of the firmament[6] of bards and sages. Yet he dismisses without notice his thought, because it is his. In every work of genius we recognize our own rejected thoughts: they come back to us with a certain alienated majesty. Great works of art have no more affecting lesson for us than this. They teach us to abide by our spontaneous impression with good-humored inflexibility then most when the whole cry of voices is on the other side. Else, to-morrow a stranger will say with masterly good sense precisely what we have thought and felt all the time, and we shall be forced to take with shame our own opinion from another.

---

1. Pronounced EHM-ih-nehnt. Note-worthy.
2. Pronounced ad-muh-NISH-uhn. Friendly warning.
3. Pronounced LAYT-ihnt. Something not visible now, but ready to reveal itself at any moment.
4. Plato (c. 427–c. 347 BC), a Greek philosopher who believed in the idea of perfect forms.
5. Milton (1608–1674), an English epic poet who wrote *Paradise Lost*.
6. Pronounced FER-muh-muhnt. Here, metaphorical "external expanse" describing the lofty ideas of storytellers (or poets) and philosophers of the day.

There is a time in every man's education when he arrives at the conviction that envy is ignorance; that imitation is suicide; that he must take himself for better, for worse, as his portion; that though the wide universe is full of good, no kernel of nourishing corn can come to him but through his toil bestowed on that plot of ground which is given to him to till. The power which resides in him is new in nature, and none but he knows what that is which he can do, nor does he know until he has tried. Not for nothing one face, one character, one fact, makes much impression on him, and another none. This sculpture in the memory is not without preëstablished harmony. The eye was placed where one ray should fall, that it might testify of that particular ray. We but half express ourselves, and are ashamed of that divine idea which each of us represents. It may be safely trusted as proportionate and of good issues, so it be faithfully imparted, but God will not have his work made manifest by cowards. A man is relieved and gay when he has put his heart into his work and done his best; but what he has said or done otherwise shall give him no peace. It is a deliverance which does not deliver. In the attempt his genius deserts him; no muse befriends; no invention, no hope.

Trust thyself: every heart vibrates to that iron string. Accept the place the divine providence has found for you, the society of your contemporaries, the connection of events. Great men have always done so, and confided themselves childlike to the genius of their age, betraying their perception that the absolutely trustworthy was seated at their heart, working through their hands, predominating in all their being. And we are now men, and must accept in the highest mind the same transcendent[7] destiny; and not minors and invalids in a protected corner, not cowards fleeing before a revolution, but guides, redeemers, and

---

7. Pronounced tran-SEHN-duhnt. Overarching, something that "goes beyond."

benefactors, obeying the Almighty effort, and advancing on Chaos[8] and the Dark.

What pretty oracles[9] nature yields us on this text, in the face and behavior of children, babes, and even brutes! That divided and rebel mind, that distrust of a sentiment because our arithmetic has computed the strength and means opposed to our purpose, these have not. Their mind being whole, their eye is as yet unconquered, and when we look in their faces we are disconcerted. Infancy conforms to nobody: all conform to it, so that one babe commonly makes four or five out of the adults who prattle and play to it. So God has armed youth and puberty and manhood no less with its own piquancy[10] and charm, and made it enviable and gracious and its claims not to be put by, if it will stand by itself. Do not think the youth has no force, because he cannot speak to you and me. Hark! in the next room his voice is sufficiently clear and emphatic. It seems he knows how to speak to his contemporaries. Bashful or bold, then, he will know how to make us seniors very unnecessary.

The nonchalance[11] of boys who are sure of a dinner, and would disdain as much as a lord to do or say aught[12] to conciliate[13] one, is the healthy attitude of human nature. A boy is in the parlor what the pit is in the playhouse;[14] independent, irresponsible, looking out from his corner on such people and facts as pass by, he tries and sentences them on their merits, in the swift, summary way of boys, as good, bad, interesting, silly, eloquent,

---

8. From the Greek "Χάος," the disorganized state of the world before harmony and reason began to reign.
9. Pronounced OR-uh-kuhlz. Here, means answers.
10. Pronounced PEEK-uhn-see. Excitement.
11. Pronounced nahn-shuh-LAHNS. Indifference, casualness.
12. Sounds like "ought." Anything.
13. Pronounced kuhn-SIHL-ee-ayt. Here, means to earn or gain (a dinner).
14. In a theater, the "pit" was the lowest and cheapest section of seats. Audience members who sat here were notoriously outspoken, even during a performance.

troublesome. He cumbers[15] himself never about consequences about interests; he gives an independent, genuine verdict. You must court him: he does not court you. But the man is, as it were, clapped into jail by his consciousness. As soon as he has once acted or spoken with *éclat*[16] he is a committed person, watched by the sympathy or the hatred of hundreds, whose affections must now enter into his account. There is no Lethe[17] for this. Ah, that he could pass again into his neutrality! Who can thus avoid all pledges, and having observed, observe again from the same unaffected, unbiased, unbribable, unaffrighted innocence, must always be formidable. He would utter opinions on all passing affairs, which being seen to be not private, but necessary, would sink like darts into the ear of men, and put them in fear.

These are the voices which we hear in solitude, but they grow faint and inaudible as we enter into the world. Society everywhere is in conspiracy against the manhood of everyone of its members. Society is a joint-stock company, in which the members agree, for the better securing of his bread to each shareholder, to surrender the liberty and culture of the eater. The virtue in most request is conformity. Self-reliance is its aversion. It loves not realities and creators, but names and customs.

Whoso would be a man must be a nonconformist. He who would gather immortal palms must not be hindered by the name of goodness, but must explore if it be goodness. Nothing is at last sacred but the integrity of your own mind. Absolve[18] you to yourself, and you shall have the suffrage[19] of the world. I remember an answer which when quite young I was prompted

---

15. Burdens.
16. Pronounced ay-CLAH. Flamboyant style and enthusiasm.
17. Pronounced LEE-thee. (*Th* as in "thick.") A mythical river in the Underworld that made people forget.
18. Pronounce ab-ZOLV. To absolve someone is to free him or her from guilt.
19. Pronounced SUFF-rihj. A vote, a voice. In this case, with a connotation of approval.

to make to a valued adviser, who was wont[20] to importune[21] me with the dear old doctrines of the church. On my saying, What have I to do with the sacredness of traditions, if I live wholly from within? my friend suggested: "But these impulses may be from below, not from above." I replied: "They do not seem to me to be such; but if I am the Devil's child, I will live then from the Devil." No law can be sacred to me but that of my nature. Good and bad are but names very readily transferable to that or this; the only right is what is after my constitution, the only wrong what is against it. A man is to carry himself in the presence of all opposition, as if everything were titular[22] and ephemeral[23] but he. I am ashamed to think how easily we capitulate[24] to badges and names, to large societies and dead institutions. Every decent and well-spoken individual affects and sways me more than is right. I ought to go upright and vital, and speak the rude truth in all ways. If malice and vanity wear the coat of philanthropy,[25] shall that pass? If an angry bigot[26] assumes this bountiful cause of Abolition, and comes to me with his last news from Barbadoes,[27] why should I not say to him: "Go love thy infant; love thy wood-chopper: be good-natured and modest: have that grace; and never varnish[28] your hard, uncharitable ambition with this incredible tenderness for black folk a thousand miles off. Thy love afar is spite at home." Rough and graceless would be such greeting, but truth is handsomer than the affectation of

---

20. Sounds like "won't" or sometimes "want." Inclined.
21. Pronounced ihm-por-TOON. Annoy, harass, press.
22. Pronounced TIH-chuh-ler. Having to do with a title. Here, seems to imply something that is only of consequence in name, not in reality.
23. Pronounced ih-FEHM-uh-ruhl. Fleeting.
24. Pronounced cuh-PIHCH-uh-layt. Give in.
25. Pronounced fuh-LAN-thruh-pee. Universal good will; the love of mankind.
26. Pronounced BIH-guht. Here, means a person stubbornly and inconsiderately devoted to his or her own beliefs.
27. Barbados, an island in the Caribbean.
28. Pronounced VAR-nish. Put a good face on, with the connotation of being dishonest by covering up the true state of something.

love. Your goodness must have some edge to it,—else it is none. The doctrine of hatred must be preached as the counteraction of the doctrine of love when that pules and whines. I shun father and mother and wife and brother, when my genius calls me. I would write on the lintels[29] of the door-post, *Whim*.[30] I hope it is somewhat better than whim at last, but we cannot spend the day in explanation. Expect me not to show cause why I seek or why I exclude company. Then, again, do not tell me, as a good man did to-day, of my obligation to put all poor men in good situations. Are they *my* poor? I tell thee, thou foolish philanthropist, that I grudge the dollar, the dime, the cent, I give to such men as do not belong to me and to whom I do not belong. There is a class of persons to whom by all spiritual affinity[31] I am bought and sold; for them I will go to prison, if need be; but your miscellaneous[32] popular charities; the education at college of fools; the building of meeting-houses[33] to the vain end to which many now stand; alms[34] to sots;[35] and the thousand-fold Relief Societies;—though I confess with shame I sometimes succumb and give the dollar, it is a wicked dollar which by and by I shall have the manhood to withhold.

8 Virtues are, in the popular estimate, rather the exception than the rule. There is the man *and* his virtues. Men do what is called a good action, as some piece of courage or charity, much as they would pay a fine in expiation[36] of daily non-appearance on parade. Their works are done as an apology or extenuation[37]

---

29. Pronounced LIHN-tuhlz. A lintel is the horizontal, top piece of a doorframe.
30. Impulse. Emerson would rather have people assume his actions are due to some "whim" than have to explain himself.
31. Pronounced uh-FIHN-ih-tee. Closeness, kinship.
32. Pronounced miss-uh-LAYN-ee-uss. Various, with a connotation of randomness.
33. Churches.
34. Pronounced ALL-mz. Money given to the poor.
35. Rhymes with "dots." Drunkards.
36. Pronounced ehks-pee-AY-shun. Atonement.
37. Pronounced ehks-tehn-yoo-AY-shun. Partial justification.

of their living in the world,—as invalids and the insane pay a high board. Their virtues are penances. I do not wish to expiate, but to live. My life is for itself and not for a spectacle. I much prefer that it should be of a lower strain, so it be genuine and equal, than that it should be glittering and unsteady. I wish it to be sound and sweet, and not to need diet and bleeding.[38] I ask primary evidence that you are a man, and refuse this appeal from the man to his actions. I know that for myself it makes no difference whether I do or forbear those actions which are reckoned excellent. I cannot consent to pay for a privilege where I have intrinsic right. Few and mean as my gifts may be, I actually am, and do not need for my own assurance or the assurance of my fellows any secondary testimony.

What I must do is all that concerns me, not what the people think. This rule, equally arduous[39] in actual and in intellectual life, may serve for the whole distinction between greatness and meanness.[40] It is the harder, because you will always find those who think they know what is your duty better than you know it. It is easy in the world to live after the world's opinion; it is easy in solitude to live after our own; but the great man is he who in the midst of the crowd keeps with perfect sweetness the independence of solitude.

The objection to conforming to usages that have become dead to you is, that it scatters your force. It loses your time and blurs the impression of your character. If you maintain a dead church, contribute to a dead Bible-society, vote with a great party either for the government or against it, spread your table like base[41] housekeepers,—under all these screens I have diffi-

---

38. "Bleeding" is a reference to the old medical practice where patients were cut and intentionally bled to get rid of "bad blood." Here, Emerson means that he doesn't want to rely on diet and medical care, generally.
39. Pronounced AR-joo-uss. Difficult, labor-intensive.
40. Lowliness.
41. Of low position in society.

SELF-RELIANCE

culty to detect the precise man you are. And, of course, so much force is withdrawn from your proper life. But do your work, and I shall know you.[42] Do your work, and you shall reinforce yourself. A man must consider what a blindman's-buff is this game of conformity. If I know your sect,[43] I anticipate your argument. I hear a preacher announce for his text and topic the expediency[44] of one of the institutions of his church. Do I not know beforehand that not possibly can he say a new and spontaneous word? Do I not know that, with all this ostentation[45] of examining the grounds of the institution, he will do no such thing? Do I not know that he is pledged to himself not to look but at one side,—the permitted side, not as a man, but as a parish minister? He is a retained attorney, and these airs of the bench[46] are the emptiest affectation. Well, most men have bound their eyes with one or another handkerchief,[47] and attached themselves to some one of these communities of opinion. This conformity makes them not false in a few particulars, authors of a few lies, but false in all particulars. Their every truth is not quite true. Their two is not the real two, their four not the real four; so that every word they say chagrins[48] us, and we know not where to begin to set them right. Meantime nature is not slow to equip us in the prison-uniform of the party to which we adhere. We come to wear one cut of face and figure, and acquire by

---

42. Matthew 7:16, 20.
43. Pronounced SEHKT. Group, particularly a group as opposed to another with different views.
44. Pronounced ehks-PEE-dee-ehn-see. Quickness and effectiveness toward a certain end.
45. Pronounced ah-stehn-TAY-shun. Something is ostentatious if it is elaborate and showy.
46. Airs of impartiality, as a judge on his or her bench might possess.
47. An allusion to Blindman's Bluff, a game of where one person is blindfolded and must try to tag the other players.
48. Pronounced shuh-GRIHNZ. Disappoints, with the connotation of annoyance and confusion.

degrees the gentlest asinine[49] expression. There is a mortifying experience in particular which does not fail to wreak itself also in the general history; I mean "the foolish face of praise," the forced smile which we put on in company where we do not feel at ease in answer to conversation which does not interest us. The muscles, not spontaneously moved, but moved by a low usurping willfulness, grow tight about the outline of the face with the most disagreeable sensation.

11 For nonconformity the world whips you with its displeasure. And therefore a man must know how to estimate a sour face. The bystanders look askance[50] on him in the public street or in the friend's parlor. If this aversation[51] had its origin in contempt and resistance like his own, he might well go home with a sad countenance; but the sour faces of the multitude, like their sweet faces, have no deep cause, but are put on and off as the wind blows and a newspaper directs. Yet is the discontent of the multitude more formidable than that of the senate and the college. It is easy enough for a firm man who knows the world to brook[52] the rage of the cultivated classes. Their rage is decorous[53] and prudent, for they are timid as being very vulnerable themselves. But when to their feminine rage the indignation of the people is added, when the ignorant and the poor are aroused, when the unintelligent brute force that lies at the bottom of society is made to growl and mow,[54] it needs the habit of magnanimity and religion to treat it godlike as a trifle of no concernment.

---

49. Pronounced ASS-ih-nine. Here, means donkey-like.
50. Pronounced uh-SKANS. To look askance at someone or something is to eye it with suspicion.
51. Pronounced uh-ver-SAY-shuhn. Act of turning away in disgust or dislike.
52. Rhymes with "look." Tolerate.
53. Pronounced DEH-kuh-russ. Proper.
54. Rhymes with "go." Grimace.

12 The other terror[55] that scares us from self-trust is our consistency; a reverence for our past act or word, because the eyes of others have no other data for computing our orbit than our past acts, and we are loath to disappoint them.

13 But why should you keep your head over your shoulder? Why drag about this corpse of your memory, lest you contradict somewhat[56] you have stated in this or that public place? Suppose you should contradict yourself; what then? It seems to be a rule of wisdom never to rely on your memory alone, scarcely even in acts of pure memory, but to bring the past for judgment into the thousand-eyed present, and live ever in a new day. In your metaphysics[57] you have denied personality to the Deity; yet when the devout motions of the soul come, yield to them heart and life, though they should clothe God with shape and color. Leave your theory, as Joseph his coat in the hand of the harlot, and flee.[58]

14 A foolish consistency is the hobgoblin of little minds, adored by little statesmen and philosophers and divines. With consistency a great soul has simply nothing to do. He may as well concern himself with the shadow on the wall.[59] Speak what you think now in hard words, and to-morrow speak what to-morrow thinks in hard words again, though it contradict everything you said to-day.—"Ah, so you shall be sure to be misunderstood."—Is it so bad, then, to be misunderstood? Pythagoras[60] was misunderstood, and Socrates,[61] and Jesus, and

---

55. The first terror is conformity.
56. Something.
57. Pronounced MEH-tuh-FIHZ-ihks. Understanding of reality.
58. Genesis 39:12.
59. Probably an allusion to Plato's Cave Analogy, in which people living in a cave believe shadows on the wall to be the "real thing," not realizing that they're mere shadows of something truly real.
60. Pronounced puh-THA-guh-russ. Pythagoras (c. 570–c. 495 BC), a Greek philosopher and mathematician, from whom we get the Pythagorean Theorem.
61. Pronounced SAH-cruh-teez. Socrates (c. 470–399 BC), a Greek philosopher who taught by asking questions, from whom we get "the Socratic method" and

Luther,[62] and Copernicus,[63] and Galileo,[64] and Newton,[65] and every pure and wise spirit that ever took flesh. To be great is to be misunderstood.

I suppose no man can violate his nature. All the sallies[66] of his will are rounded in by the law of his being, as the inequalities of Andes[67] and Himmaleh[68] are insignificant in the curve of the sphere. Nor does it matter how you gauge and try him. A character is like an acrostic[69] or Alexandrian stanza;[70]—read it forward, backward, or across, it still spells the same thing. In this pleasing, contrite wood-life which God allows me, let me record day by day my honest thought without prospect or retrospect, and, I cannot doubt, it will be found symmetrical, though I mean it not, and see it not. My book should smell of pines and resound with the hum of insects. The swallow over my window should interweave that thread or straw he carries in his bill into my web also. We pass for what we are. Character teaches above our wills. Men imagine that they communicate their virtue or vice only by overt actions, and do not see that virtue or vice emit a breath every moment.

"Socratic dialogue."
62. Martin Luther (1483–1546), a German theologian who began the Protestant Reformation.
63. Nicolaus Copernicus (1473–1543), a German astronomer and mathematician who suggested that the sun was the center of the universe.
64. Galileo Galilei (1564–1642), an Italian astronomer who was put under house arrest by the Catholic Church for "heresy," holding beliefs that opposed those of the Church.
65. Isaac Newton (1642–1727), an English scientist who "discovered" gravity.
66. Ventures.
67. A mountain range in South America.
68. The Himalayas are a mountain range in Asia.
69. A poem where, taken together, the first letter of every line spells out a word.
70. An Alexandrian line is a line with twelve syllables, every other one being stressed. This pattern is called "iambic hexameter." Neither an Alexandrian stanza nor an acrostic actually read the same forward and backward as Emerson suggests here. Emerson may be thinking of a palindrome.

16

There will be an agreement in whatever variety of actions, so they be each honest and natural in their hour. For of one will, the actions will be harmonious, however unlike they seem. These varieties are lost sight of at a little distance, at a little height of thought. One tendency unites them all. The voyage of the best ship is a zigzag line of a hundred tacks.[71] See the line from a sufficient distance, and it straightens itself to the average tendency. Your genuine action will explain itself, and will explain your other genuine actions. Your conformity explains nothing. Act singly, and what you have already done singly will justify you now. Greatness appeals to the future. If I can be firm enough to-day to do right, and scorn eyes,[72] I must have done so much right before as to defend me now. Be it how it will, do right now. Always scorn appearances, and you always may. The force of character is cumulative. All the foregone days of virtue work their health into this. What makes the majesty of the heroes of the senate and the field, which so fills the imagination? The consciousness of a train of great days and victories behind. They shed an united light on the advancing actor. He is attended as by a visible escort of angels. That is it which throws thunder into Chatham's[73] voice, and dignity into Washington's port, and America into Adams's[74] eye. Honor is venerable[75] to us because it is no ephemeris.[76] It is always ancient virtue. We worship it to-day because it is not of to-day. We love it and pay it homage, because it is not a trap for our love and homage, but is

---

71. "Tacking" is the act of sailing in a zigzag pattern.
72. To ignore people who are watching.
73. William Pitt, Earl of Chatham (1708–1778), an English statesman and public speaker, known for his rhetorical skill.
74. Samuel Adams (1722–1803), American revolutionary and member of the Continental Congress, or John Adams (1735–1826), the United States' second president.
75. Pronounced VEHN-er-uh-bull. Wise and respected.
76. Pronounced eh-FEHM-er-iss. An account of daily transactions or a chart that plots heavenly bodies. Emerson may also mean that honor is not ephemeral (i.e., not fleeting).

self-dependent, self-derived, and therefore of an old immaculate[77] pedigree,[78] even if shown in a young person.

I hope in these days we have heard the last of conformity and consistency. Let the words be gazetted[79] and ridiculous henceforward. Instead of the gong for dinner, let us hear a whistle from the Spartan[80] fife. Let us never bow and apologize more. A great man is coming to eat at my house. I do not wish to please him; I wish that he should wish to please me. I will stand here for humanity, and though I would make it kind, I would make it true. Let us affront and reprimand the smooth mediocrity and squalid[81] contentment of the times, and hurl in the face of custom, and trade, and office, the fact which is the upshot of all history, that there is a great responsible Thinker and Actor working wherever a man works; that a true man belongs to no other time or place, but is the center of things. Where he is, there is nature. He measures you, and all men, and all events. Ordinarily, everybody in society reminds us of somewhat else, or of some other person. Character, reality, reminds you of nothing else; it takes place of the whole creation. The man must be so much, that he must make all circumstances indifferent. Every true man is a cause, a country, and an age; requires infinite spaces and numbers and time fully to accomplish his design;—and posterity seem to follow his steps as a train of clients. A man Cæsar is born, and for ages after we have a Roman Empire. Christ is born, and millions of minds so grow and cleave[82] to his genius, that he is confounded with virtue and the possible of man. An institution is the lengthened

---

77. Pronounced ih-MA-kyuh-liht. Pure.
78. Pronounced PEH-duh-gree. Background, ancestry.
79. Pronounced guh-ZEHT'd. Announced to the public.
80. The Spartans were famously courageous and well-trained.
81. Pronounced SKWAH-lihd. Disgusting.
82. Rhymes with "leave." Here, means hold, adhere.

shadow of one man; as Monachism,[83] of the hermit Antony;[84] the Reformation,[85] of Luther; Quakerism,[86] of Fox;[87] Methodism, of Wesley;[88] Abolition, of Clarkson.[89] Scipio,[90] Milton called "the height of Rome"; and all history resolves itself very easily into the biography of a few stout and earnest persons.

Let a man then know his worth, and keep things under his feet. Let him not peep or steal, or skulk up and down with the air of a charity-boy, a bastard, or an interloper, in the world which exists for him. But the man in the street, finding no worth in himself which corresponds to the force which built a tower or sculptured a marble god, feels poor when he looks on these. To him a palace, a statue, a costly book, have an alien and forbidding air, much like a gay equipage, and seem to say like that, "Who are you, Sir?" Yet they all are his, suitors for his notice, petitioners to his faculties that they will come out and take possession. The picture waits for my verdict: it is not to command me, but I am to settle its claims to praise. That popular fable[91] of the sot who was picked up dead drunk in the street, carried to the duke's house, washed and dressed and laid in the duke's bed, and, on his waking, treated with all obsequious[92] ceremony like the duke, and assured that he had been insane,

---

83. Pronounced MAHN-uh-kihz-uhm. A synonym for monasticism, being a monk.
84. Saint Anthony or Anthony the Great (c. 251–356), the Egyptian founder of monasticism.
85. The Protestant Reformation, started by Martin Luthur in 1517.
86. Quakers, named for their tendency to "quake" during worship, are a sect of Christianity, founded by George Fox (1624–1691), that believes in peace and inner light.
87. George Fox (1624–1691), an Englishman who started Quakerism.
88. John Wesley (1703–1791), an Englishman who founded Methodism.
89. Thomas Clarkson (1760–1846), an English abolitionist.
90. Scipio Africanus (c. 235–c. 184 BC), a Roman general who defeated Hannibal at the Battle of Zama (202 BC).
91. An allusion to two pieces of literature: *Arabian Nights* and *The Taming of the Shrew*, wherein a sleepy or drunk man is put in a lord's place.
92. Pronounced uhb-SEE-kwee-uss. Adoring in a submissive, over-the-top way.

owes its popularity to the fact that it symbolizes so well the state of man, who is in the world a sort of sot, but now and then wakes up, exercises his reason, and finds himself a true prince.

Our reading is mendicant[93] and sycophantic.[94] In history, our imagination plays us false. Kingdom and lordship, power and estate, are a gaudier[95] vocabulary than private John and Edward in a small house and common day's work; but the things of life are the same to both; the sum total of both is the same. Why all this deference to Alfred,[96] and Scanderbeg,[97] and Gustavus?[98] Suppose they were virtuous; did they wear out virtue? As great a stake depends on your private act to-day, as followed their public and renowned steps. When private men shall act with original views, the luster will be transferred from the actions of kings to those of gentlemen.

The world has been instructed by its kings, who have so magnetized the eyes of nations. It has been taught by this colossal symbol the mutual reverence that is due from man to man. The joyful loyalty with which men have everywhere suffered the king, the noble, or the great proprietor to walk among them by a law of his own, make his own scale of men and things, and reverse theirs, pay for benefits not with money but with honor, and represent the law in his person, was the hieroglyphic[99] by which they obscurely signified their consciousness of their own right and comeliness, the right of every man.

---

93. Pronounced MEHN-dih-kuhnt. Reduced to begging.
94. Pronounced sih-kuh-FAN-tihk. Obsequious.
95. Pronounced GAW-dee-er. Something is gaudy when it's glitzy and showy in a tacky way.
96. Alfred the Great (c. 849–901), a Saxon king and scholar.
97. Also known as George Castriota (1405–1467), an Albanian military leader who fought for Christianity against the Turks.
98. Gustav II Adolf (1594–1632), a Swedish king who used the Thirty Years' War (1618–1648) to establish Sweden as a great power.
99. Pronounced hy-roe-GLIHF-ihk. A symbol needing to be deciphered. From the Egyptian written language of symbols, or hieroglyphics.

The magnetism which all original action exerts is explained when we inquire the reason of self-trust. Who is the Trustee? What is the aboriginal[100] Self, on which a universal reliance may be grounded? What is the nature and power of that science-baffling star, without parallax,[101] without calculable elements, which shoots a ray of beauty even into trivial and impure actions, if the least mark of independence appear? The inquiry leads us to that source, at once the essence of genius, of virtue, and of life, which we call Spontaneity or Instinct. We denote this primary wisdom as Intuition, whilst all later teachings are tuitions. In that deep force, the last fact behind which analysis cannot go, all things find their common origin. For the sense of being which in calm hours rises, we know not how, in the soul, is not diverse from things, from space, from light, from time, from man, but one with them, and proceeds obviously from the same source whence their life and being also proceed. We first share the life by which things exist, and afterwards see them as appearances in nature, and forget that we have shared their cause. Here is the fountain of action and of thought. Here are the lungs of that inspiration which giveth man wisdom, and which cannot be denied without impiety and atheism. We lie in the lap of immense intelligence, which makes us receivers of its truth and organs of its activity. When we discern justice, when we discern truth, we do nothing of ourselves, but allow a passage to its beams. If we ask whence this comes, if we seek to pry into the soul that causes, all philosophy is at fault. Its presence or its absence is all we can affirm. Every man discriminates between the voluntary acts of his mind, and his involuntary perceptions, and knows that to his involuntary perceptions a perfect faith is due. He may err in the expression of them, but he knows that these things are so, like day and night, not to be disputed.

---

100. Pronounced ab-uh-RIHJ-uh-null. First, original.
101. Pronounced PEHR-uh-laks. A method used by astronomers to measure distances between objects in the sky.

My willful actions and acquisitions are but roving;—the idlest reverie, the faintest native emotion, command my curiosity and respect. Thoughtless people contradict as readily the statement of perceptions as of opinions, or rather much more readily; for, they do not distinguish between perception and notion. They fancy that I choose to see this or that thing. But perception is not whimsical, it is fatal. If I see a trait, my children will see it after me, and in course of time, all mankind,—although it may chance that no one has seen it before me. For my perception of it is as much a fact as the sun.

The relations of the soul to the divine spirit are so pure, that it is profane to seek to interpose[102] helps. It must be that when God speaketh he should communicate, not one thing, but all things; should fill the world with his voice; should scatter forth light, nature, time, souls, from the center of the present thought; and new date and new create the whole. Whenever a mind is simple, and receives a divine wisdom, old things pass away,— means, teachers, texts, temples, fall; it lives now, and absorbs past and future into the present hour. All things are made sacred by relation to it,—one as much as another. All things are dissolved to their center by their cause, and, in the universal miracle, petty and particular miracles disappear. If, therefore, a man claims to know and speak of God, and carries you backward to the phraseology of some old moldered[103] nation in another country, in another world, believe him not. Is the acorn better than the oak which is its fullness and completion? Is the parent better than the child into whom he has cast his ripened being? Whence, then, this worship of the past? The centuries are conspirators against the sanity and authority of the soul. Time and space are but physiological colors which the eye makes, but the soul is light; where it is, is day; where it was, is night; and history is

---

102. Pronounced ihn-ter-POSE. ("Pose" rhymes with "chose.") Interrupt with.
103. Pronounced MOLE-der'd. Deteriorated.

an impertinence and an injury, if it be anything more than a cheerful apologue[104] or parable of my being and becoming.

Man is timid and apologetic; he is no longer upright; he dares not say "I think," "I am,"[105] but quotes some saint or sage. He is ashamed before the blade of grass or the blowing rose. These roses under my window make no reference to former roses or to better ones; they are for what they are; they exist with God to-day. There is no time to them. There is simply the rose; it is perfect in every moment of its existence. Before a leaf-bud has burst, its whole life acts; in the full-blown flower there is no more; in the leafless root there is no less. Its nature is satisfied, and it satisfies nature, in all moments alike. But man postpones, or remembers; he does not live in the present, but with a reverted eye laments the past, or, heedless of the riches that surround him, stands on tiptoe to foresee the future. He cannot be happy and strong until he too lives with nature in the present, above time.

This should be plain enough. Yet see what strong intellects dare not yet hear God himself, unless he speak the phraseology of I know not what David, or Jeremiah, or Paul. We shall not always set so great a price on a few texts, on a few lives. We are like children who repeat by rote[106] the sentences of grandames[107] and tutors, and, as they grow older, of the men and talents and characters they chance to see,—painfully recollecting the exact words they spoke; afterwards, when they come into the point of view which those had who uttered those saying, they understand them, and are willing to let the words go; for, at any time, they can use words as good when occasion comes. If we live truly,

---

104. Pronounced AP-uh-log. Allegory.
105. This may be an allusion to philosopher René Descartes' famous justification for believing in his own existence: "I think, therefore I am."
106. Rhymes with "boat." To repeat "by rote" is to repeat straight from memory without any real thought.
107. Old women, grandmothers.

we shall see truly. It is as easy for the strong man to be strong, as it is for the weak to be weak. When we have new perception, we shall gladly disburden the memory of its hoarded treasures as old rubbish. When a man lives with God, his voice shall be as sweet as the murmur of the brook and the rustle of the corn.

And now at last the highest truth on this subject remains unsaid; probably cannot be said; for all that we say is the far-off remembering of the intuition. That thought, by what I can now nearest approach to say it, is this. When good is near you, when you have life in yourself, it is not by any known or accustomed way; you shall not discern the footprints of any other; you shall not see the face of man; you shall not hear any name;—the way, the thought, the good, shall be wholly strange and new. It shall exclude example and experience. You take the way from man, not to man. All persons that ever existed are its forgotten ministers. Fear and hope are alike beneath it. There is somewhat low even in hope. In the hour of vision, there is nothing that can be called gratitude, nor properly joy. The soul raised over passion beholds identity and eternal causation, perceives the self-existence of Truth and Right, and calms itself with knowing that all things go well. Vast spaces of nature, the Atlantic Ocean, the South Sea,—long intervals of time, years, centuries,—are of no account. This which I think and feel underlay every former state of life and circumstances, as it does underlie my present, and what is called life, and what is called death.

Life only avails, not the having lived. Power ceases in the instant of repose; it resides in the moment of transition from a past to a new state, in the shooting of the gulf, in the darting to an aim. This one fact the world hates, that the soul *becomes*; for that forever degrades the past, turns all riches to poverty, all reputation to shame, confounds the saint with the rogue, shoves Jesus and Judas equally aside. Why, then, do we prate[108]

---

108. Rhymes with "gate." Chatter.

of self-reliance? Inasmuch as the soul is present, there will be power not confident but agent.[109] To talk of reliance is a poor external way of speaking. Speak rather of that which relies, because it works and is. Who has more obedience than I masters me, though he should not raise his finger. Round him I must revolve by the gravitation of spirits. We fancy it rhetoric, when we speak of eminent virtue. We do not yet see that virtue is Height, and that a man or a company of men, plastic and permeable[110] to principles, by the law of nature must overpower and ride all cities, nations, kings, rich men, poets, who are not.

This is the ultimate fact which we so quickly reach on this, as on every topic, the resolution of all into the ever-blessed One. Self-existence is the attribute of the Supreme Cause, and it constitutes the measure of good by the degree in which it enters into all lower forms. All things real are so by so much virtue as they contain. Commerce, husbandry,[111] hunting, whaling, war eloquence, personal weight, are somewhat, and engage my respect as examples of its presence and impure action. I see the same law working in nature for conservation and growth. Power is in nature the essential measure of right. Nature suffers nothing to remain in her kingdoms which cannot help itself. The genesis and maturation of a planet, its poise[112] and orbit, the bended tree recovering itself from the strong wind, the vital resources of every animal and vegetable, are demonstrations of the self-sufficing, and therefore self-relying soul.

Thus all concentrates: let us not rove; let us sit at home with the cause. Let us stun and astonish the intruding rabble of men and books and institutions, by a simple declaration of the divine fact. Bid the invaders take the shoes from off their feet, for God

---

109. Active.
110. Pronounced PER-mee-uh-bull. Leaky. "Plastic and permeable" probably means "easily manipulated and with too open a mind."
111. Farming.
112. Rhymes with "noise." Here, means position of balanced equilibrium.

is here within.[113] Let our simplicity judge them, and our docility to our own law demonstrate the poverty of nature and fortune beside our native riches.

But now we are a mob. Man does not stand in awe of man, nor is his genius admonished to stay at home to put itself in communication with the internal ocean, but it goes abroad to beg a cup of water of the urns of other men. We must go alone. I like the silent church before the service begins, better than any preaching. How far off, how cool, how chaste the persons look, begirt[114] each one with a precinct[115] or sanctuary! So let us always sit. Why should we assume the faults of our friend, or wife, or father, or child, because they sit around our hearth, or are said to have the same blood? All men have my blood, and I have all men's. Not for that will I adopt their petulance or folly, even to the extent of being ashamed of it. But your isolation must not be mechanical, but spiritual, that is, must be elevation. At times the whole world seems to be in conspiracy to importune you with emphatic trifles. Friend, client, child, sickness, fear, want, charity, all knock at once at thy closet door, and say, "Come out unto us." But keep thy state; come not into their confusion. The power men possess to annoy men, I give them by a weak curiosity. No man can come near me but through my act. "What we love that we have, but by desire we bereave ourselves of the love."

If we cannot at once rise to the sanctities of obedience and faith, let us at least resist our temptations; let us enter into the state of war, and wake Thor and Woden,[116] courage and constancy, in our Saxon[117] breasts. This is to be done in our smooth times by speaking the truth. Check this lying hospitality

---

113. An allusion to removing one's shoes before entering a holy place.
114. Pronounced bih-GERT. Surround.
115. Pronounced PREE-seenkt. Enclosure.
116. Norse gods, son and father, respectively.
117. The Germanic people who came to England in the fifth century; people of English descent.

and lying affection. Live no longer to the expectation of these deceived and deceiving people with whom we converse. Say to them, O father, O mother, O wife, O brother, O friend, I have lived with you after appearances hitherto. Henceforward I am the truth's. Be it known unto you that henceforward I obey no law less than the eternal law. I will have no covenants but proximities. I shall endeavor to nourish my parents, to support my family, to be the chaste[118] husband of one wife,—but these relations I must fill after a new and unprecedented way. I appeal from your customs. I must be myself. I cannot break myself any longer for you, or you. If you can love me for what I am, we shall be the happier. If you cannot, I will still seek to deserve that you should. I will not hide my tastes or aversions. I will so trust that what is deep is holy, that I will do strongly before the sun and moon whatever inly[119] rejoices me, and the heart appoints. If you are noble, I will love you; if you are not, I will not hurt you and myself by hypocritical attentions. If you are true, but not in the same truth with me, cleave to your companions; I will seek my own. I do this not selfishly, but humbly and truly. It is alike your interest, and mine, and all men's however long we have dwelt in lies, to live in truth. Does this sound harsh to-day? You will soon love what is dictated by your nature as well as mine, and, if we follow the truth, it will bring us out safe at last. But so may you give these friends pain. Yes, but I cannot sell my liberty and my power, to save their sensibility. Besides, all persons have their moments of reason, when they look out into the region of absolute truth; then will they justify me, and do the same thing.

The populace think that your rejection of popular standards is a rejection of all standard, and mere antinomianism;[120] and

---

118. Rhymes with "waist." Pure and right, often specifically in the context of sex.
119. Internally.
120. Pronounced an-tih-NOE-mee-uhn-ihz-uhm. An extreme belief that Christians saved by grace are not obligated to obey moral law; the opposite of extreme legalism.

the bold sensualist[121] will use the name of philosophy to gild his crimes. But the law of consciousness abides. There are two confessionals, in one or the other of which we must be shriven.[122] You may fulfill your round of duties by clearing yourself in the *direct*, or in the *reflex* way. Consider whether you have satisfied your relations to father, mother, cousin, neighbor, town, cat, and dog; whether any of these can upbraid you. But I may also neglect this reflex standard, and absolve me to myself. I have my own stern claims and perfect circle. It denies the name of duty to many offices that are called duties. But if I can discharge its debts, it enables me to dispense with the popular code. If any one imagines that this law is lax, let him keep its commandment one day.

And truly it demands something godlike in him who has cast off the common motives of humanity, and has ventured to trust himself for a taskmaster. High be his heart, faithful his will, clear his sight, that he may in good earnest be doctrine, society, law, to himself, that a simple purpose may be to him as strong as iron necessity is to others!

If any man consider the present aspects of what is called by distinction *society*, he will see the need of these ethics. The sinew[123] and heart of man seem to be drawn out, and we are become timorous, desponding whimperers. We are afraid of truth, afraid of fortune, afraid of death, and afraid of each other. Our age yields no great and perfect persons. We want men and women who shall renovate life and our social state, but we see that most natures are insolvent, cannot satisfy their own wants, have an ambition out of all proportion to their practical force, and do lean and beg day and night continually. Our housekeeping is mendicant, our arts, our occupations, our marriages, our religion, we have not chosen, but society has chosen for us.

---

121. One who overly prioritizes the pleasure of the senses.
122. Pronounced SHRIH-vehn. Absolved of guilt; forgiven.
123. Pronounced SEHN-yoo. Tendons, muscles. Metaphorically refers to strength.

We are parlor soldiers. We shun the rugged battle of fate, where strength is born.

If our young men miscarry in their first enterprises, they lose all heart. If the young merchant fails, men say he is *ruined*. If the finest genius studies at one of our colleges, and is not installed in an office within one year afterwards in the cities or suburbs of Boston or New York, it seems to his friends and to himself that he is right in being disheartened, and in complaining the rest of his life. A sturdy lad from New Hampshire or Vermont, who in turn tries all the professions, who *teams it, farms it, peddles,* keeps a school, preaches, edits a newspaper, goes to Congress, buys a township, and so forth, in successive years, and always, like a cat, falls on his feet, is worth a hundred of these city dolls. He walks abreast with his days, and feels no shame in not "studying a profession," for he does not postpone his life, but lives already. He has not one chance, but a hundred chances. Let a Stoic open the resources of man, and tell men they are not leaning willows, but can and must detach themselves; that with the exercise of self-trust, new powers shall appear; that a man is the word made flesh,[124] born to shed healing to the nations, that he should be ashamed of our compassion, and that the moment he acts from himself, tossing the laws, the books, idolatries and customs out of the window, we pity him no more, but thank and revere him,—and that teacher shall restore the life of man to splendor, and make his name dear to all history.

It is easy to see that a greater self-reliance must work a revolution in all the offices and relations of men; in their religion; in their education; in their pursuits; their modes of living; their association; in their property; in their speculative views.

1. In what prayers do men allow themselves! That which they call a holy office is not so much as brave and manly. Prayer looks abroad and asks for some foreign addition to come

---

124. An allusion to Jesus, the Word made flesh (John 1:14).

through some foreign virtue, and loses itself in endless mazes of natural and supernatural, and mediatorial and miraculous. Prayer that craves a particular commodity,—anything less than all good,—is vicious. Prayer is the contemplation of the facts of life from the highest point of view. It is the soliloquy[125] of a beholding and jubilant soul. It is the spirit of God pronouncing his works good. But prayer as a means to effect a private end is meanness and theft. It supposes dualism and not unity in nature and consciousness. As soon as the man is at one with God, he will not beg. He will then see prayer in all action. The prayer of the farmer kneeling in his field to weed it, the prayer of the rower kneeling with the stroke of his oar, are true prayers heard throughout nature, though for cheap ends. Caratach, in Fletcher's *Bonduca*,[126] when admonished to inquire the mind of the god Audate, replies,—

37
"His hidden meaning lies in our endeavors;
Our valors are our best gods."

38
Another sort of false prayers are our regrets. Discontent is the want of self-reliance; it is infirmity of will. Regret calamities, if you can thereby help the sufferer; if not, attend your own work, and already the evil begins to be repaired. Our sympathy is just as base. We come to them who weep foolishly, and sit down and cry for company, instead of imparting to them truth and health in rough electric shocks,[127] putting them once more in communication with their own reason. The secret of fortune is joy in our hands. Welcome evermore to gods and men is the self-helping man. For him all doors are flung wide: him all

---

125. Pronounced suh-LIHL-uh-kwee. A speech to oneself, with a connotation of eloquence.
126. *Bonduca* is a play by John Fletcher about the Celtic queen Boudica. Caratach is a character in the play.
127. A reference to electro-shock therapy.

tongues greet, all honors crown, all eyes follow with desire. Our love goes out to him and embraces him, because he did not need it. We solicitously[128] and apologetically caress and celebrate him, because he held on his way and scorned our disapprobation.[129] The gods love him because men hated him. "To the persevering mortal," said Zoroaster,[130] "the blessed Immortals are swift."

As men's prayers are a disease of the will, so are their creeds a disease of the intellect. They say with those foolish Israelites, "Let not God speak to us, lest we die. Speak thou, speak any man with us, and we will obey."[131] Everywhere I am hindered of meeting God in my brother, because he has shut his own temple doors, and recites fables merely of his brother's, or his brother's brother's God. Every new mind is a new classification. If it prove a mind of uncommon activity and power, a Locke,[132] a Lavoisier,[133] a Hutton,[134] a Bentham,[135] a Fourier,[136] it imposes its classification on other men, and lo! a new system. In proportion to the depth of the thought, and so to the number of the objects it touches and brings within reach of the pupil, is his complacency. But chiefly is this apparent in creeds and churches, which are also classifications of some powerful mind acting on the elemental thought of duty, and man's relation to the Highest.

---

128. Pronounced suh-LISS-uh-tuss-lee. Apprehensively.
129. Pronounced diss-a-proe-BAY-shun. (*A* as in "cat.") Disapproval.
130. A Persian philosopher who lived c. 1500–1000 BC. Zoroaster believed in self-realization.
131. Exodus 20:19; Deuteronomy 5:25–27.
132. John Locke (1632–1704), an English philosopher who believed that each person is born a *tabula rasa* (Latin for "blank slate") with no innate ideas.
133. Antoine Lavoisier (luh-vwahz-YAY) (1743–1794), a French chemist who discovered the composition of water.
134. James Hutton (1726–1797), a Scottish geologist.
135. Jeremy Bentham (1748–1832), an English legislative reformer.
136. Charles Fourier (1772–1837), a French philosopher who believed that society should be composed of small, self-sufficient communities.

Such is Calvinism,[137] Quakerism,[138] Swedenborgism.[139] The pupil takes the same delight in subordinating everything to the new terminology, as a girl who has just learned botany[140] in seeing a new earth and new seasons thereby. It will happen for a time, that the pupil will find his intellectual power has grown by the study of his master's mind. But in all unbalanced minds, the classification is idolized, passes for the end, and not for a speedily exhaustible means, so that the walls of the system blend to their eye in the remote horizon with the walls of the universe; the luminaries of heaven seem to them hung on the arch their master built. They cannot imagine how you aliens have any right to see,—how you can see; "It must be somehow that you stole the light from us." They do not yet perceive that light, unsystematic, indomitable, will break into any cabin, even into theirs. Let them chirp awhile and call it their own. If they are honest and do well, presently their neat new pinfold will be too straight and low, will crack, will lean, will rot and vanish, and the immortal light, all young and joyful, million-orbed, million-colored, will beam over the universe as on the first morning.

40

2. It is for want of self-culture that the superstition of Traveling, whose idols are Italy, England, Egypt, retains its fascination for all educated Americans. They who made England, Italy, or Greece venerable in the imagination did so by sticking fast where they were, like an axis of the earth. In manly hours, we feel that duty is our place. The soul is no traveler; the wise man stays at home, and when his necessities, his duties, on any occasion call him from his house, or into foreign lands, he is at home still; and shall make men sensible by the expression of

---

137. A type of Protestantism founded by John Calvin (1509–1564). Calvinists believe in salvation by faith and that people are predestined either to become saved or not.
138. See footnote on page 21.
139. Founded by Emmanuel Swedenborg (1688–1772), Swedenborgists believe that Jesus was not the Son of God, but God himself. Swedenborg also claimed to have had mystical encounters with Christ.
140. Pronounced BAH-tuh-nee. The study of plants.

his countenance, that he goes the missionary of wisdom and virtue, and visits cities and men like a sovereign, and not like an interloper or a valet.

41 I have no churlish[141] objection to the circumnavigation of the globe, for the purposes of art, of study, and benevolence, so that the man is first domesticated, or does not go abroad with the hope of finding somewhat greater than he knows. He who travels to be amused, or to get somewhat which he does not carry, travels away from himself, and grows old even in youth among old things. In Thebes,[142] in Palmyra,[143] his will and mind have become old and dilapidated as they. He carries ruins to ruins.

42 Traveling is a fool's paradise. Our first journeys discover to us the indifference of places. At home I dream that at Naples, at Rome, I can be intoxicated with beauty, and lose my sadness. I pack my trunk, embrace my friends, embark on the sea, and at last wake up in Naples, and there beside me is the stern fact, the sad self, unrelenting, identical, that I fled from. I seek the Vatican,[144] and the palaces. I affect to be intoxicated with sights and suggestions, but I am not intoxicated. My giant goes with me wherever I go.

43 3. But the rage of traveling is a symptom of a deeper unsoundness affecting the whole intellectual action. The intellect is vagabond,[145] and our system of education fosters restlessness. Our minds travel when our bodies are forced to stay at home. We imitate; and what is imitation but the traveling of the mind? Our houses are built with foreign taste; our shelves

---

141. Rhymes with "girlish." Surly, disapproving in a petty way.
142. Emerson may be referring to Thebes, Greece, or Thebes, Egypt. Both cities were ruined, so his meaning remains the same either way.
143. A city in Syria, also called Tadmor, possibly built by King Solomon (2 Chronicles 8:4; 1 Kings 9:17–19.)
144. This city-state in Rome is the headquarters of the Roman Catholic Church, and where the Pope lives.
145. Pronounced VA-guh-bahnd. Wandering, with a negative connotation.

are garnished with foreign ornaments; our opinions, our tastes, our faculties, lean, and follow the Past and the Distant. The soul created the arts wherever they have flourished. It was in his own mind that the artist sought his model. It was an application of his own thought to the thing to be done and the conditions to be observed. And why need we copy the Doric[146] or the Gothic[147] model? Beauty, convenience, grandeur of thought, and quaint expression are as near to us as to any, and if the American artist will study with hope and love the precise thing to be done by him considering the climate, the soil, the length of the day, the wants of the people, the habit and form of the government, he will create a house in which all these will find themselves fitted, and taste and sentiment will be satisfied also.

44 Insist on yourself; never imitate. Your own gift you can present every moment with the cumulative force of a whole life's cultivation; but of the adopted talent of another, you have only an extemporaneous,[148] half possession. That which each can do best, none but his Maker can teach him. No man yet knows what it is, nor can, till that person has exhibited it. Where is the master who could have taught Shakespeare? Where is the master who could have instructed Franklin, or Washington, or Bacon,[149] or Newton? Every great man is a unique. The Scipionism of Scipio is precisely that part he could not borrow. Shakespeare will never be made by the study of Shakespeare. Do that which is assigned to you, and you cannot hope too much or dare too much. There is at this moment for you an utterance brave and grand as that of the colossal chisel of Phidias,[150] or trowel of the Egyptians, or

---

146. An ancient Greek style of architecture, characterized by its simplicity.
147. A medieval European style of architecture, characterized by flying buttresses and pointed arches.
148. Pronounced eks-tehm-puh-RAY-nee-uss. Unplanned, impromptu. From the Latin *ex*, meaning "out of" and *tempus*, meaning "time."
149. Francis Bacon (1561–1626), an English philosopher who established the scientific method.
150. Phidias (c. 490–430 BC), a Greek sculptor.

the pen of Moses, or Dante,[151] but different from all these. Not possibly will the soul all rich, all eloquent, with thousand-cloven tongue, deign[152] to repeat itself; but if you can hear what these patriarchs say, surely you can reply to them in the same pitch of voice; for the ear and the tongue are two organs of one nature. Abide in the simple and noble regions of thy life, obey thy heart, and thou shalt reproduce the Foreworld again.

4. As our Religion, our Education, our Art look abroad, so does our spirit of society. All men plume themselves on the improvement of society, and no man improves.

Society never advances. It recedes as fast on one side as it gains on the other. It undergoes continual changes; it is barbarous, it is civilized, it is Christianized, it is rich, it is scientific; but this change is not amelioration.[153] For everything that is given, something is taken. Society acquires new arts, and loses old instincts. What a contrast between the well-clad, reading, writing, thinking American, with a watch, a pencil, and a bill of exchange in his pocket, and the naked New Zealander, whose property is a club, a spear, a mat, and an undivided twentieth of a shed to sleep under! But compare the health of the two men, and you shall see that the white man has lost his aboriginal strength. If the traveler tell us truly, strike the savage with a broad ax, and in a day or two the flesh shall unite and heal as if you struck the blow into soft pitch, and the same blow shall send the white to his grave.

The civilized man has built a coach, but has lost the use of his feet. He is supported on crutches, but lacks so much support of muscle. He has a fine Geneva watch,[154] but he fails of the skill

---

151. Dante Alighieri (1265–1321), an Italian epic poet who wrote *The Divine Comedy*, a trilogy of books telling the allegorical story of himself journeying through the afterlife.
152. Rhymes with "plane." To allow reluctantly.
153. Pronounced uh-mee-lee-uh-RAY-shun. To ameliorate is to make better, easier, less painful.
154. Geneva is a city in Switzerland.

to tell the hour by the sun. A Greenwich nautical almanac he has, and so being sure of the information when he wants it, the man in the street does not know a star in the sky. The solstice he does not observe; the equinox he knows as little; and the whole bright calendar of the year is without a dial in his mind. His notebooks impair his memory; his libraries overload his wit; the insurance office increases the number of accidents; and it may be a question whether machinery does not encumber; whether we have not lost by refinement some energy, by a Christianity entrenched in establishments and forms, some vigor of wild virtue. For every Stoic was a Stoic; but in Christendom where is the Christian?

There is no more deviation in the moral standard than in the standard of height or bulk. No greater men are now than ever were. A singular equality may be observed between great men of the first and of the last ages; nor can all the science, art, religion, and philosophy of the nineteenth century avail to educate greater men than Plutarch's[155] heroes, three or four and twenty centuries ago. Not in time is the race progressive. Phocion,[156] Socrates, Anaxagoras,[157] Diogenes,[158] are great men, but they leave no class. He who is really of their class will not be called by their name, but will be his own man, and, in his turn, the founder of a sect. The arts and inventions of each period are only its costume, and do not invigorate men. The harm of the improved machinery may compensate its good. Hudson[159]

---

155. Pronounced PLOO-tark (c. AD 46–120), a Greek philosopher who wrote a series of Greek and Roman biographies.
156. Phocion (402–317 BC), an Athenian politician and military leader.
157. Anaxagoras (500–426 BC), a Greek philosopher who lived and worked before Socrates.
158. Diogenes (c. 404–323 BC), a Greek philosopher who shunned wealth and comfort.
159. Henry Hudson (1565–1611), an English explorer who discovered the Hudson Bay.

and Bering[160] accomplished so much in their fishing boats, as to astonish Parry[161] and Franklin,[162] whose equipment exhausted the resources of science and art. Galileo, with an opera-glass, discovered a more splendid series of celestial phenomena than any one since. Columbus found the New World in an undecked boat. It is curious to see the periodical disuse and perishing of means and machinery, which were introduced with loud laudation[163] a few years or centuries before. The great genius returns to essential man. We reckoned the improvements of the art of war among the triumphs of science, and yet Napoleon conquered Europe by the bivouac,[164] which consisted of falling back on naked valor, and disencumbering it of all aids. The Emperor held it impossible to make a perfect army, says Las Cases,[165] "without abolishing our arms, magazines, commissaries,[166] and carriages, until, in imitation of the Roman custom, the soldier should receive his supply of corn, grind it in his handmill, and bake his bread himself."

Society is a wave. The wave moves onward, but the water of which it is composed does not. The same particle does not rise from the valley to the ridge. Its unity is only phenomenal. The persons who make up a nation to-day, next year die, and their experience with them.

And so the reliance on Property, including the reliance on governments which protect it, is the want of self-reliance. Men have looked away from themselves and at things so long, that they have come to esteem the religious, learned, and civil

---
160. Vitus Bering (1680–1741), a Danish explorer who discovered the Bering Strait.
161. William Parry (1790–1855), an English explorer of the Arctic.
162. John Franklin (1786–1847), an English explorer who was lost and died while exploring the Arctic.
163. Pronounced law-DAY-shun. Praise. From the Latin *laudare* meaning "to praise."
164. Pronounced BIH-vuh-wak. A camp made for just one night, often without tents.
165. Emmanuel, comte de las Cases (1766–1842), a French atlas-maker and author of *Mémorial de Sainte-Hélène*, a text chronicling and admiring Napoleon.
166. Pronounced KAH-mih-sehr-eez. Pages, people sent to do small tasks.

institutions as guards of property, and they deprecate assaults on these, because they feel them to be assaults on property. They measure their esteem of each other by what each has, and not by what each is. But a cultivated man becomes ashamed of his property, out of new respect for his nature. Especially he hates what he has, if he see that it is accidental,—came to him by inheritance, or gift, or crime; then he feels that it is not having; it does not belong to him, has no root in him, and merely lies there, because no revolution or no robber takes it away. But that which a man is, does always by necessity acquire, and what the man acquires is living property, which does not wait the beck[167] of rulers, or mobs, or revolutions, or fire, or storm, or bankruptcies, but perpetually renews itself wherever the man breathes. "Thy lot or portion of life," said the Caliph Ali,[168] "is seeking after thee; therefore be at rest from seeking after it." Our dependence on these foreign goods leads us to our slavish respect for numbers. The political parties meet in numerous conventions; the greater the concourse, and with each new uproar of announcement, The delegation from Essex! The Democrats from New Hampshire! The Whigs of Maine! the young patriot feels himself stronger than before by a new thousand of eyes and arms. In like manner the reformers summon conventions, and vote and resolve in multitude. Not so, O friends! will the god deign to enter and inhabit you, but by a method precisely the reverse. It is only as a man puts off all foreign support, and stands alone, that I see him to be strong and to prevail. He is weaker by every recruit to his banner. Is not a man better than a town? Ask nothing of men, and in the endless mutation, thou only firm column must presently appear the upholder of all that surrounds thee. He who knows that power is inborn, that he

---

167. Rhymes with "neck." Short for beckon. "To wait at the beck" is to stand ready for someone (usually a bossy or unreasonable someone) to give you a task.
168. Ali was a relative of Mohammed. A caliph (pronounced CA-lihf) is the ruler of a Muslim state.

is weak because he has looked for good out of him and elsewhere, and so perceiving, throws himself unhesitatingly on his thought, instantly rights himself, stands in the erect position, commands his limbs, works miracles; just as a man who stands on his feet is stronger than a man who stands on his head.

So use all that is called Fortune. Most men gamble with her, and gain all, and lose all, as her wheel rolls. But do thou leave as unlawful these winnings, and deal with Cause and Effect, the chancelors of God. In the Will work and acquire, and thou hast chained the wheel of Chance, and shalt sit hereafter out of fear from her rotations. A political victory, a rise of rents, the recovery of your sick, or the return of your absent friend, or some other favorable event, raises your spirits, and you think good days are preparing for you. Do not believe it. Nothing can bring you peace but yourself. Nothing can bring you peace but the triumph of principles.

Self-Reliance and Essays on the Nature of Man

Emerson House, Concord, MA

— 1842 *death* of a son

— 1840s *buys* 11 acres on Walden Pond

— 1842 an experimental utopian community farm, "Fruitlands" is formed nearby by Bronson Alcott and Charles Lane, fellow transcendentalists. The farm is abandoned in 1844.

"I will not prejudge them successful. They look well in July—we will see them in December. ...Their manners and behavior in the house and in the field were those of superior men—of men at rest."
—Emerson's journal entry, July 8 as quoted by B. F. Sanborn in *Bronson Alcott at Alcott house, England, and Fruitlands, New England (1842–1844)*

— 1844 *publishes* Essays (second series)

— 1847 *tours* Britain; seeks out Thomas Carlyle in Scotland

"Philosophy complains that Custom has hoodwinked us, from the first; that we do everything by Custom, even Believe by it; that our very Axioms, let us boast of Free-thinking as we may, are oftenest simply such Beliefs as we have never heard questioned. Nay, what is Philosophy throughout but a continual battle against Custom; an ever-renewed effort to transcend the sphere of blind Custom, and so become Transcendental?"
—Thomas Carlyle in Book 3, Chapter 8 of *Sartor Resartus* (1833–1834)

— 1850 *publishes* "Shakspeare" in *Representative Men*

SHAKSPEARE
or, The Poet

GREAT men are more distinguished by range and extent than by originality. If we require the originality which consists in weaving, like a spider, their web from their own bowels; in finding clay and making bricks and building the house; no great men are original. Nor does valuable originality consist in unlikeness to other men. The hero is in the press of knights and the thick of events; and seeing what men want and sharing their desire, he adds the needful length of sight and of arm, to come at the desired point. The greatest genius is the most indebted man. A poet is no rattle-brain, saying what comes uppermost, and, because he says every thing, saying at last something good; but a heart in unison with his time and country. There is nothing whimsical and fantastic in his production, but sweet and sad earnest, freighted with the weightiest convictions and pointed with the most determined aim which any man or class knows of in his times.

The Genius of our life is jealous of individuals, and will not have any individual great, except through the general. There is no choice to genius. A great man does not wake up on some fine morning and say, "I am full of life, I will go to sea and find an Antarctic continent: to-day I will square the circle: I will ransack botany and find a new food for man: I have a new architecture in my mind: I foresee a new mechanic power:" no, but he finds himself in the river of the thoughts and events, forced onward by the ideas and necessities of his contemporaries. He stands where all the eyes of men look one way, and their hands all point in the direction in which he should go. The Church has reared him amidst rites[1] and pomps,[2] and he carries out the advice which her music gave him, and builds a cathedral needed by her chants and processions. He finds a war raging: it educates him, by trumpet, in barracks,[3] and he betters the instruction. He finds two counties groping to bring coal, or flour, or fish, from the place of production to the place of consumption, and he hits on a railroad. Every master has found his materials collected, and his power lay in his sympathy with his people and in his love of the materials he wrought in. What an economy of power! and what a compensation for the shortness of life! All is done to his hand. The world has brought him thus far on his way. The human race has gone out before him, sunk the hills, filled the hollows and bridged the rivers. Men, nations, poets, artisans, women, all have worked for him, and he enters into their labors. Choose any other thing, out of the line of tendency, out of the national feeling and history, and he would have all to do for himself: his powers would be expended in the first preparations. Great genial[4] power, one would almost say, consists in not being original at all; in being altogether receptive; in letting the world do all, and suffering the spirit of the hour to pass unobstructed through the mind.

---

1. Sounds like "rights." Rituals.
2. Pronounced PAHMPS. Showy displays.
3. Pronounced BEHR-eks. Military housing.
4. Pronounced JEE-nee-uhl. Here, means natural, original, or creative (power), but genial can also refer to contributing to propagation, giving cheerfulness, or supporting life.

Shakspeare's[5] youth fell in a time when the English people were importunate for dramatic entertainments. The court took offence easily at political allusions[6] and attempted to suppress them. The Puritans,[7] a growing and energetic party, and the religious among the Anglican church, would suppress them. But the people wanted them. Inn-yards, houses without roofs, and extemporaneous enclosures at country fairs were the ready theatres of strolling players. The people had tasted this new joy; and, as we could not hope to suppress newspapers now,—no, not by the strongest party,—neither then could king, prelate,[8] or puritan, alone or united, suppress an organ[9] which was ballad,[10] epic, newspaper, caucus,[11] lecture, Punch[12] and library, at the same time. Probably king, prelate and puritan, all found their own account in it. It had become, by all causes, a national interest,—by no means conspicuous, so that some great scholar would have thought of treating it in an English history,—but not a whit less considerable because it was cheap and of no account, like a baker's-shop. The best proof of its vitality is the crowd of writers which suddenly broke into this field; Kyd,

---

5. "Shakespeare" is spelled as Shakspeare and as Shakespeare in this essay. We have kept the original spellings.
6. Pronounced uh-LOO-zjuhnz. Indirect references to another literary work, historical figure, or event.
7. A group of Protestants who intentionally broke away from the Church of England and were therefore very against and sensitive to icons, elaborate ceremony, or anything they perceived to be showy.
8. Pronounced PREHL-iht. A religious official, like a bishop.
9. Here, a natural instrument of action or operation.
10. Pronounced BA-lihd. A poem meant to be set to music.
11. Pronounced KAW-kuhs. A meeting of people of the same political party to discuss policy or select the party's candidate.
12. The main character of a puppet show. Here, Emerson is using the figure of speech "synecdoche," in which part of something is used to represent the whole thing. In this case, "Punch" is used to mean puppet shows as a whole.

Marlow, Greene, Jonson, Chapman, Dekker, Webster, Heywood, Middleton, Peele, Ford, Massinger, Beaumont and Fletcher.[13]

The secure possession, by the stage, of the public mind, is of the first importance to the poet who works for it. He loses no time in idle experiments. Here is audience and expectation prepared. In the case of Shakspeare there is much more. At the time when he left Stratford[14] and went up to London, a great body of stage-plays of all dates and writers existed in manuscript and were in turn produced on the boards. Here is the Tale of Troy[15], which the audience will bear hearing some part of, every week; the Death of Julius Cæsar, and other stories out of Plutarch, which they never tire of; a shelf full of English history, from the chronicles of Brut and Arthur,[16] down to the royal Henries,[17] which men hear eagerly; and a string of doleful[18] tragedies, merry Italian tales and Spanish voyages, which all the London 'prentices[19] know. All the mass has been treated, with more or less skill, by every playwright, and the prompter has the soiled and tattered manuscripts. It is now no longer possible to

---

13. All dramatists of the English Renaissance. They competed fiercely to sell their plays to the wealthy owners of permanent playhouses, such as the Globe, the Rose, and the Swan, which were located outside London. Thomas Kyd (1558–1594); Christopher Marlowe (1564–1593); Robert Greene (c. 1558–1592); Ben Jonson (c. 1572–1637); George Chapman (c. 1559–1634); Thomas Dekker (c. 1572–1632); John Webster (c. 1578–1626); Thomas Heywood (c. 1575–1641); Thomas Middleton (1580–1627); George Peele (c. 1556–1596); John Ford (c. 1586–1639); Philip Massinger (c. 1583–1640); Francis Beaumont (c. 1585–1616); John Fletcher (1579–1625).
14. Probably the mid-1580s.
15. *Many* classic works dealt with the Trojan War.
16. Brutus of Troy and King Arthur were two legendary or mythical British kings of different eras that were immortalized in priest Layamon's poem *Brut* (c. 1190), a chronicle of British history.
17. England's kings named Henry were the subject of many historical plays, including those by Shakespeare. Henry IV, V, and VI were particularly famous. These "Henries" ruled in succession from 1399 to 1471 as the House of Lancaster.
18. Pronounced DOLE-ful. Sorrowful.
19. Apprentices.

say who wrote them first. They have been the property of the Theatre so long, and so many rising geniuses have enlarged or altered them, inserting a speech or a whole scene, or adding a song, that no man can any longer claim copyright in this work of numbers. Happily, no man wishes to. They are not yet desired in that way. We have few readers, many spectators and hearers. They had best lie where they are.

Shakspeare, in common with his comrades, esteemed the mass of old plays waste stock, in which any experiment could be freely tried. Had the *prestige*[20] which hedges about a modern tragedy existed, nothing could have been done. The rude warm blood of the living England circulated in the play, as in street-ballads, and gave body which he wanted to his airy and majestic fancy. The poet needs a ground in popular tradition on which he may work, and which, again, may restrain his art within the due temperance. It holds him to the people, supplies a foundation for his edifice,[21] and in furnishing so much work done to his hand, leaves him at leisure and in full strength for the audacities of his imagination. In short, the poet owes to his legend what sculpture owed to the temple. Sculpture in Egypt and in Greece grew up in subordination to architecture. It was the ornament of the temple wall: at first a rude relief carved on pediments,[22] then the relief became bolder and a head or arm was projected from the wall; the groups being still arranged with reference to the building, which serves also as a frame to hold the figures; and when at last the greatest freedom of style and treatment was reached, the prevailing genius of architecture

---

20. Pronounced prehs-TEEJ. Acclaim, high esteem. Until the mid-1800s, the term referred to magic or trickery. Around Emerson's time, it shifted to take on the meaning of "reputation."
21. Pronounced EHD-ih-fiss. A building.
22. Pronounced PEH-dih-ments. A pediment is a triangle-shaped area at the top of a Greek building that faces outward and usually features figures carved "in relief," meaning they are halfway emerging from the stone from which they're carved.

still enforced a certain calmness and continence[23] in the statue. As soon as the statue was begun for itself, and with no reference to the temple or palace, the art began to decline: freak, extravagance and exhibition took the place of the old temperance. This balance-wheel,[24] which the sculptor found in architecture, the perilous irritability of poetic talent found in the accumulated dramatic materials to which the people were already wonted,[25] and which had a certain excellence which no single genius, however extraordinary, could hope to create.

6 In point of fact it appears that Shakspeare did owe debts in all directions, and was able to use whatever he found; and the amount of indebtedness may be inferred from Malone's[26] laborious computations in regard to the First, Second and Third parts of *Henry VI.*, in which, "out of 6043 lines, 1771 were written by some author preceding Shakspeare, 2373 by him, on the foundation laid by his predecessors, and 1899 were entirely his own."[27] And the proceeding investigation hardly leaves a single drama of his absolute invention. Malone's sentence is an important piece of external history. In *Henry VIII.* I think I see plainly the cropping out of the original rock on which his own finer stratum[28] was laid. The first play was written by a superior, thoughtful man, with a vicious ear. I can mark his lines, and

---

23. Pronounced KAHN-tih-nuhns. Sense of self-control.
24. A time-keeping device similar to a pendulum, but wheel-shaped. Here, Emerson is using "balance-wheel" as a metaphor for how poetry and sculpture need to be grounded in something (history or architecture) and pulled back toward that center.
25. Pronounced like "wanted." Here, Emerson is using the word to mean "inclined."
26. Edmond Malone (1741–1812), an Irish-born English scholar who analyzed and edited works of Shakespeare.
27. From *A Dissertation on the Three Parts of King Henry VI* by Edmond Malone, London: Henry Baldwin Press, 1787.
28. Layer.

know well their cadence[29]. See Wolsey's[30] soliloquy, and the following scene with Cromwell,[31] where instead of the metre of Shakspeare, whose secret is that the thought constructs the tune, so that reading for the sense will best bring out the rhythm,—here the lines are constructed on a given tune, and the verse has even a trace of pulpit eloquence. But the play contains through all its length unmistakable traits of Shakspeare's hand, and some passages, as the account of the coronation, are like autographs. What is odd, the compliment to Queen Elizabeth is in the bad rhythm.

Shakspeare knew that tradition supplies a better fable than any invention can. If he lost any credit of design, he augmented his resources; and, at that day, our petulant demand for originality was not so much pressed. There was no literature for the million. The universal reading, the cheap press, were unknown. A great poet who appears in illiterate times, absorbs into his sphere all the light which is any where radiating. Every intellectual jewel, every flower of sentiment it is his fine office to bring to his people; and he comes to value his memory equally with his invention. He is therefore little solicitous whence his thoughts have been derived; whether through translation, whether through tradition, whether by travel in distant countries, whether by inspiration; from whatever source, they are equally welcome to his uncritical audience. Nay, he borrows very near home. Other men say wise things as well as he; only they say a good many foolish things, and do not know when they have spoken wisely. He knows the sparkle of the true stone, and puts it in high place, wherever he finds it. Such is the happy

---

29. Pronounced KAY-dehns. Rhythym, with regard to speech or music. Cadence has a pleasant, lyrical connotation.
30. Cardinal Thomas Wolsey (1473–1530), a real historical figure and character in Shakespeare's *Henry VIII*. A cardinal is an official of the Catholic Church just below the pope.
31. Thomas Cromwell (c. 1485–1540), another real figure and character in *Henry VIII*. Cromwell was chief minister to King Henry VIII.

position of Homer[32] perhaps; of Chaucer,[33] of Saadi[34]. They felt that all wit was their wit. And they are librarians and historiographers, as well as poets. Each romancer was heir and dispenser of all the hundred tales of the world,—

> "Presenting Thebes' and Pelops' line
> And the tale of Troy divine."[35]

The influence of Chaucer is conspicuous in all our early literature; and more recently not only Pope and Dryden[36] have been beholden to him, but, in the whole society of English writers, a large unacknowledged debt is easily traced. One is charmed with the opulence[37] which feeds so many pensioners. But Chaucer is a huge borrower. Chaucer, it seems, drew continually, through Lydgate and Caxton,[38] from Guido di Colonna, whose Latin romance of the Trojan war was in turn a compilation from Dares Phrygius,[39] Ovid and Statius[40]. Then Petrarch,[41]

---

32. Homer (c. 800 BC), a Greek epic poet, who wrote *The Iliad* and *The Odyssey*, the stories of the Trojan War and general Odysseus's journey home, respectively.
33. Geoffrey Chaucer (c. 1343–1400), an Old English poet, who wrote *The Canterbury Tales*.
34. Saadi Shirazi (1210–1291), a medieval Persian poet who was nicknamed "Master of Speech."
35. From the poem *Il Penseroso* by John Milton (1608–1674).
36. Alexander Pope (1688–1744, an English satirical poet; John Dryden (1631–1700), an English poet and playwright and England's first "poet laureate," or royally appointed official poet of the country.
37. Pronounced AHP-yuh-lunce. Wealth, usually with the connotation of being visible or tangible.
38. Emerson's timeline seems slightly muddled here. William Caxton (c. 1422–1491), a translator and printer (born after Chaucer's death) brought the story of Troy into English from French. He was also responsible for printing the works of Chaucer and John Lydgate (c. 1370–1449), an English poet contemporary with Chaucer.
39. In Chaucer's *House of Fame* Book III, he mentions that he is striving to be equal to Guido di Colonna and Dares Phrygius, two ancient authors, the former Sicilian, the latter Greek.
40. Ovid (c. 43 BC–AD 17) and Statius (45–96), both Roman poets.
41. Full name Francesco Petrarca (1304–1374), an Italian Renaissance poet and humanist, i.e., someone who believes that mankind and its accomplishments are the most important things (rather than God or religion).

Boccaccio[42] and the Provençal poets[43] are his benefactors: the Romaunt of the Rose is only judicious translation from William of Lorris and John of Meung[44]: Troilus and Creseide, from Lollius of Urbino: The Cock and the Fox, from the *Lais* of Marie: The House of Fame, from the French or Italian: and poor Gower he uses as if he were only a brick-kiln or stone-quarry out of which to build his house. He steals by this apology,[45]—that what he takes has no worth where he finds it and the greatest where he leaves it. It has come to be practically a sort of rule in literature, that a man having once shown himself capable of original writing, is entitled thenceforth to steal from the writings of others at discretion. Thought is the property of him who can entertain it and of him who can adequately place it. A certain awkwardness marks the use of borrowed thoughts; but as soon as we have learned what to do with them they become our own.

Thus all originality is relative. Every thinker is retrospective. The learned member of the legislature, at Westminster or at Washington,[46] speaks and votes for thousands. Show us the constituency,[47] and the now invisible channels by which the senator is made aware of their wishes; the crowd of practical and knowing men, who, by correspondence or conversation, are feeding him with evidence, anecdotes[48] and estimates, and

---

42. Giovanni Boccaccio (c. 1313–1375), an Italian poet known for *The Decameron*, a collection of novellas (very short novels).
43. This term refers to the literature of southern France in the eleventh and twelfth centuries, which influenced famous figures such as Dante and Petrarch.
44. Here Emerson names the medieval sources that Chaucer used for his poems *The Romaunt of the Rose* (c. 1360), *Troilus and Creseyde* (c. 1380), the cock and the fox in "The Nun's Priest's Tale" (c. 1390, part of *The Canterbury Tales*), and *The House of Fame* (c. 1379).
45. Explanation.
46. Two nation capitals (Westminster being an area of London).
47. Pronounced kuhn-STIH-choo-ehn-see. The group of people represented by an elected person.
48. Pronounced AN-ehk-dotes. Short, engaging stories relevant to a point.

it will bereave[49] his fine attitude and resistance of something of their impressiveness. As Sir Robert Peel and Mr. Webster vote,[50] so Locke and Rousseau[51] think, for thousands; and so there were fountains all around Homer, Menu,[52] Saadi, or Milton, from which they drew; friends, lovers, books, traditions, proverbs,—all perished—which, if seen, would go to reduce the wonder. Did the bard speak with authority? Did he feel himself overmatched by any companion? The appeal is to the consciousness of the writer. Is there at last in his breast a Delphi[53] whereof to ask concerning any thought or thing, whether it be verily so, yea or nay? and to have answer, and to rely on that? All the debts which such a man could contract to other wit would never disturb his consciousness of originality; for the ministrations of books and of other minds are a whiff of smoke to that most private reality with which he has conversed.

11   It is easy to see that what is best written or done by genius in the world, was no man's work, but came by wide social labor, when a thousand wrought like one, sharing the same impulse. Our English Bible is a wonderful specimen of the strength and music of the English language. But it was not made by one man, or at one time; but centuries and churches brought it to perfection. There never was a time when there was not some

---

49. Pronounced buh-REEV. Strip away, with a connotation of grief.
50. Peel (1788–1850), a conservative English statesman; Daniel Webster (1782–1852), American Secretary of State and infamous supporter of the Fugitive Slave Law of 1850.
51. John Locke (see footnote on page 33); Jean-Jacques Rousseau (1712–1778), a French Enlightenment philosopher. Emerson compares government officials, such as Robert Peel and Daniel Webster, who do not speak for themselves when they vote, to philosophers. In doing so, he claims that philosophers are not expressing original ideas either.
52. In Hindu myth, Manu Vaivasvata was an Indian king who built a boat to survive the Great Flood and save the *Vedas*, a collection of four sacred texts.
53. Pronounced DELL-fie. ("Fie" rhymes with "die.") A sactuary on Mount Parnassus, Greece; or, in this case, the oracle (prophetess) who lived there.

translation existing. The Liturgy,[54] admired for its energy and pathos,[55] is an anthology of the piety of ages and nations, a translation of the prayers and forms of the Catholic church,—these collected, too, in long periods, from the prayers and meditations of every saint and sacred writer all over the world. Grotius[56] makes the like remark in respect to the Lord's Prayer,[57] that the single clauses of which it is composed were already in use in the time of Christ, in the Rabbinical[58] forms. He picked out the grains of gold. The nervous language of the Common Law,[59] the impressive forms of our courts and the precision and substantial truth of the legal distinctions, are the contribution of all the sharp-sighted, strong-minded men who have lived in the countries where these laws govern. The translation of Plutarch gets its excellence by being translation on translation. There never was a time when there was none. All the truly idiomatic[60] and national phrases are kept, and all others successively picked out and thrown away. Something like the same process had gone on, long before, with the originals of these books. The world takes liberties with world-books. Vedas, Æsop's Fables,[61]

---

54. Pronounced LIHT-er-jee. The ritual form of words and actions used for Christian worship.
55. Pronounced PA-thoes or PAY-thoes (*th* as in "thick"; *oes* as in "dose"). One of Aristotle's three methods of persuasion: *logos* (reason), *pathos* (emotion), and *ethos* (the morality/authority of the speaker).
56. Hugo Grotius (1583–1645), a Dutch theologian, poet, and statesman who studied natural law and helped shape international law.
57. Matthew 6:9–13.
58. Having to do with a Rabbi, a Jewish religious teacher.
59. Law based on past precedent; the body of law formed by judges' decisions over time.
60. Pronounced ihd-ee-uh-MA-tihk. Marked by idioms: patterns or figures of speech specific to a language/culture.
61. A collection of animal fables written by the Greek slave Aesop around the fifth or sixth century BC.

Pilpay,[62] Arabian Nights,[63] Cid,[64] *Iliad*,[65] *Robin Hood*,[66] Scottish Minstrelsy,[67] are not the work of single men. In the composition of such works the time thinks, the market thinks, the mason, the carpenter, the merchant, the farmer, the fop,[68] all think for us. Every book supplies its time with one good word; every municipal law,[69] every trade, every folly of the day; and the generic catholic genius who is not afraid or ashamed to owe his originality to the originality of all, stands with the next age as the recorder and embodiment of his own.

We have to thank the researches of antiquaries, and the Shakspeare Society, for ascertaining the steps of the English drama, from the Mysteries[70] celebrated in churches and by churchmen, and the final detachment from the church, and the completion of secular plays, from Ferrex and Porrex,[71] and *Gammer Gurton's Needle*,[72] down to the possession of the stage by the very pieces which Shakspeare altered, remodelled and finally made his own. Elated with success and piqued[73] by the growing interest of the problem, they have left no bookstall unsearched, no chest in a garret[74] unopened, no file of old yellow accounts to decompose in damp and worms, so keen was the

---

62. The "Fables of Pilpay" is a translation of a collection of animal fables from India that was widely translated and distributed in the Middle Ages and earlier.
63. A famous collection of Middle Eastern stories.
64. *El Cantar de Mio Cid*, an epic poem from medieval Spain.
65. See footnote for Homer on page 50.
66. The story of the legendary British outlaw who robbed the rich to give to the poor.
67. A collection of Scottish ballads.
68. A man who is vain about his appearance and clothes; a dandy.
69. Pronounced myoo-NISS-ih-pull. The law of a particular city.
70. A genre of play that portrays the lives of saints.
71. Two brothers and princes who vie for the throne in Thomas Norton (1532–1584) and Thomas Sackville's (1536–1608) play *Gorboduc*.
72. One of the earliest English comedy plays, possibly written by John Still (c. 1543–1607).
73. Pronounced PEEK'd. Interested, drawn in by.
74. Rhymes with "carrot." An attic; a room on the highest floor of the house.

hope to discover whether the boy Shakspeare poached[75] or not, whether he held horses at the theatre door, whether he kept school, and why he left in his will only his second-best bed to Ann Hathaway, his wife.

13 There is somewhat touching in the madness with which the passing age mischooses the object on which all candles shine and all eyes are turned; the care with which it registers every trifle touching Queen Elizabeth and King James, and the Essexes, Leicesters, Burleighs and Buckinghams[76]; and lets pass without a single valuable note the founder of another dynasty, which alone will cause the Tudor dynasty[77] to be remembered,— the man who carries the Saxon[78] race in him by the inspiration which feeds him, and on whose thoughts the foremost people of the world are now for some ages to be nourished, and minds to receive this and not another bias. A popular player;—nobody suspected he was the poet of the human race; and the secret was kept as faithfully from poets and intellectual men as from courtiers[79] and frivolous people. Bacon, who took the inventory of the human understanding for his times, never mentioned his name. Ben Jonson,[80] though we have strained his few words of regard and panegyric,[81] had no suspicion of the elastic fame whose first

---

75. Rhymes with "coached." Hunted illegally.
76. English Queen Elizabeth I (1533–1603); King James VI of Scotland and I of England and Ireland (1566–1625); Walter Devereux, Earl of Essex, and his son Robert were great friends of Elizabeth I; Robert Dudley, Earl of Leicester (rhymes with "Chester"), was also a friend and suitor of Elizabeth I's; William Cecil, Baron of Burghley, was Elizabeth I's chief minister (an informal position, not to be confused with Prime Minister), Secretary of State, and later the Lord High Treasurer; George Villiers, Duke of Buckingham, was a friend of James I and Charles I..
77. Rulers of England from 1485–1603, under Henry VII, Henry VIII, Edward VI, Mary I, and Elizabeth I.
78. See footnote on page 28.
79. Pronounced KOR-tee-erz. Attendants in a royal court. Courtiers are people important enough to be around royalty but are not royalty themselves.
80. Jonson (1572–1637), an English literary critic and playwright.
81. Pronounced pan-uh-JEER-ihk. A written or spoken piece that honors someone's life.

vibrations he was attempting. He no doubt thought the praise he has conceded to him generous, and esteemed himself, out of all question, the better poet of the two.

14

If it need wit to know wit, according to the proverb, Shakspeare's time should be capable of recognizing it. Sir Henry Wotton[82] was born four years after Shakspeare, and died twenty-three years after him; and I find, among his correspondents and acquaintances, the following persons: Theodore Beza, Isaac Casaubon, Sir Philip Sidney, the Earl of Essex, Lord Bacon, Sir Walter Raleigh, John Milton, Sir Henry Vane, Isaac Walton, Dr. Donne, Abraham Cowley, Bellarmine, Charles Cotton, John Pym, John Hales, Kepler, Vieta, Albericus Gentilis, Paul Sarpi, Arminius; with all of whom exists some token of his having communicated, without enumerating many others whom doubtless he saw,—Shakspeare, Spenser, Jonson, Beaumont, Massinger, the two Herberts, Marlow, Chapman and the rest[83]. Since the constellation of great men who appeared in Greece in the time of Pericles,[84] there was never any such society;— yet their genius failed them to find out the best head in the universe. Our poet's mask was impenetrable. You cannot see the mountain near. It took a century to make it suspected; and not until two centuries had passed, after his death, did any criticism which we think adequate begin to appear. It was not possible to write the history of Shakspeare till now; for he is the father of German literature: it was with the introduction of Shakspeare into German, by Lessing,[85] and the translation of his works by

---

82. Wotton (1568–1639), an English author and ambassador who said, "An ambassador is an honest man sent to lie abroad for the commonwealth."
83. These notable names—philosophers, theologians, poets, scientists—would have been familiar to Emerson's audience. All are examples of the kind of "wits" that Emerson says should have been able to recognize Shakespeare's wit.
84. Pericles (494 BC–429), an Athenian politician and leader during the Peloponnesian Wars.
85. Gotthold Ephraim Lessing (1729–1781) urged his German countrymen to use Shakespeare's works as an inspiration and model of good playwriting.

Wieland and Schlegel,[86] that the rapid burst of German literature was most intimately connected. It was not until the nineteenth century, whose speculative genius is a sort of living Hamlet,[87] that the tragedy of Hamlet could find such wondering readers. Now, literature, philosophy and thought are Shakspearized. His mind is the horizon beyond which, at present, we do not see. Our ears are educated to music by his rhythm. Coleridge and Goethe[88] are the only critics who have expressed our convictions with any adequate fidelity: but there is in all cultivated minds a silent appreciation of his superlative power and beauty, which, like Christianity, qualifies the period.

The Shakspeare Society[89] have inquired in all directions, advertised the missing facts, offered money for any information that will lead to proof,—and with what result? Beside some important illustration of the history of the English stage, to which I have adverted, they have gleaned a few facts touching the property, and dealings in regard to property, of the poet. It appears that from year to year he owned a larger share in the Blackfriars' Theatre[90]: its wardrobe and other appurtenances[91] were his: that he bought an estate in his native village with his

---

86. Christoph Martin Wieland (1733–1813) translated twenty-two of Shakespeare's play into prose (prose is literature that is not poetry or plays). August Wilhelm Schlegel (1767–1845), a German poet and critic whose German translations of Shakespeare are noted for capturing the unique brilliance of Shakespeare. They are considered some of the best works in translation to ever be produced.
87. The hero of Shakespeare's *Hamlet*, written around 1600.
88. Samuel Taylor Coleridge (1772–1834), an English poet and philosopher. Johann Wolfgang von Goethe (1749–1832), a German writer and politician.
89. This society lasted from 1840–1853. The New Shakspere [sic] Society was founded in 1873.
90. Shakespeare's plays were performed at the second Blackfriars theatre, built by James Burbage (c. 1531–1597). Shakespeare, along with six other men, was a shareholder. It was approximately a hundred feet long and fifty feet wide, with two-story galleries along the sides for the nobility and space for commoners in front of the stage ("the pit"). Blackfriars was one of the first theaters to use artificial lighting and music between acts.
91. Pronounced uh-PER-tih-nuns-ehz. Accessories.

earnings as writer and shareholder; that he lived in the best house in Stratford; was intrusted by his neighbors with their commissions in London, as of borrowing money, and the like; that he was a veritable[92] farmer. About the time when he was writing *Macbeth*, he sues Philip Rogers,[93] in the borough-court of Stratford, for thirty-five shillings, ten pence,[94] for corn delivered to him at different times; and in all respects appears as a good husband, with no reputation for eccentricity or excess. He was a good-natured sort of man, an actor and shareholder in the theatre, not in any striking manner distinguished from other actors and managers. I admit the importance of this information. It was well worth the pains that have been taken to procure it.

16

But whatever scraps of information concerning his condition these researches may have rescued, they can shed no light upon that infinite invention which is the concealed magnet of his attraction for us. We are very clumsy writers of history. We tell the chronicle of parentage, birth, birth-place, schooling, school-mates, earning of money, marriage, publication of books, celebrity, death; and when we have come to an end of this gossip, no ray of relation appears between it and the goddess-born; and it seems as if, had we dipped at random into the "Modern Plutarch," and read any other life there, it would have fitted the poems as well. It is the essence of poetry to spring, like the rainbow daughter of Wonder, from the invisible, to abolish the past and refuse all history. Malone, Warburton, Dyce and Collier[95] have wasted their oil. The famed theatres, Covent Garden, Drury Lane, the Park and Tremont[96] have vainly assisted. Betterton, Garrick, Kemble, Kean and

---

92. Pronounced VEHR-ih-tuh-bull. Honest-to-goodness.
93. This court case is Rogers' only claim to "fame."
94. About $315 today.
95. Scholars who edited Shakespeare.
96. Famous theaters of the eighteenth and nineteenth centuries.

Macready[97] dedicate their lives to this genius; him they crown, elucidate,[98] obey and express. The genius knows them not. The recitation begins; one golden word leaps out immortal from all this painted pedantry[99] and sweetly torments us with invitations to its own inaccessible homes. I remember I went once to see the *Hamlet* of a famed performer, the pride of the English stage; and all I then heard and all I now remember of the tragedian was that in which the tragedian had no part; simply Hamlet's question to the ghost:—

> "What may this mean,
> That thou, dead corse, again in complete steel
> Revisit'st thus the glimpses of the moon?"[100]

That imagination which dilates the closet he writes in to the world's dimension, crowds it with agents in rank and order, as quickly reduces the big reality to be the glimpses of the moon. These tricks of his magic spoil for us the illusions of the green-room[101]. Can any biography shed light on the localities into which the Midsummer Night's Dream admits me? Did Shakspeare confide to any notary[102] or parish recorder, sacristan[103], or surrogate in Stratford, the genesis of that delicate creation? The forest of Arden,[104] the nimble air of Scone Castle,[105]

---

97. Famous actors who performed in Shakespeare plays.
98. Pronounced ih-LOO-sih-dayt. Shed light on. From the Latin *e*, meaning "out of," and *lux*, meaning "light."
99. Pronounced PEHD-uhn-tree. A pretentious or showy display of knowledge.
100. *Hamlet*, Act I Scene 4.
101. The lounge for performers when they are not needed on stage.
102. Pronounced NOE-tuh-ree. A person officially certified to witness document signings.
103. Pronounced SAK-rih-stun. A sexton; someone in charge of the church building and equipment.
104. The setting Shakespeare's play *As You Like It*.
105. Emerson probably means Inverness, a different Scottish castle, where *Macbeth* is set.

the moonlight of Portia's villa,[106] "the antres [107]vast and desarts idle"[108] of Othello's captivity,—where is the third cousin, or grand-nephew, the chancellor's file of accounts, or private letter, that has kept one word of those transcendent secrets? In fine, in this drama, as in all great works of art,—in the Cyclopæan architecture of Egypt and India,[109] in the Phidian sculpture, the Gothic minsters, the Italian painting, the Ballads of Spain and Scotland,—the Genius draws up the ladder after him, when the creative age goes up to heaven, and gives way to a new age, which sees the works and asks in vain for a history.

18 Shakspeare is the only biographer of Shakspeare; and even he can tell nothing, except to the Shakspeare in us, that is, to our most apprehensive and sympathetic hour. He cannot step from off his tripod and give us anecdotes of his inspirations. Read the antique documents extricated,[110] analyzed and compared by the assiduous[111] Dyce and Collier,[112] and now read one of these skyey[113] sentences,—aerolites,[114]—which seem to have fallen out of heaven, and which not your experience but the man within the breast has accepted as words of fate, and tell me if they match; if the former account in any manner for the latter; or which gives the most historical insight into the man.

---

106. From Shakespeare's *Merchant of Venice*.
107. Pronounced AN-terz. Caves.
108. *Othello*, Act I Scene 3.
109. Emerson suggests that the architecture of these countries is so large and grand it must've taken giants, Greek Cyclopses, to erect.
110. Pronounced EHKS-trih-kayt-ehd. Untangled.
111. Pronounced uh-SIHD-joo-uss. Extremely attentive and careful.
112. Alexander Dyce (1798–1869), a Scottish drama editor and historian. John Payne Collier (1789–1883), Shakespearean critic who later forged and pretended to discover documents concerning Shakespeare.
113. Pronounced SKIE-ee. Ethereal, of the sky.
114. Pronounced EHR-uh-lites. Meteorites.

SHAKSPEARE, OR THE POET

19

Hence, though our external history is so meagre, yet, with Shakspeare for biographer, instead of Aubrey[115] and Rowe,[116] we have really the information which is material; that which describes character and fortune, that which, if we were about to meet the man and deal with him, would most import us to know. We have his recorded convictions on those questions which knock for answer at every heart,—on life and death, on love, on wealth and poverty, on the prizes of life and the ways whereby we come at them; on the characters of men, and the influences, occult[117] and open, which affect their fortunes; and on those mysterious and demoniacal powers which defy our science and which yet interweave their malice and their gift in our brightest hours. Who ever read the volume of the Sonnets without finding that the poet had there revealed, under masks that are no masks to the intelligent, the lore of friendship and of love; the confusion of sentiments in the most susceptible, and, at the same time, the most intellectual of men? What trait of his private mind has he hidden in his dramas? One can discern, in his ample pictures of the gentleman and the king, what forms and humanities pleased him; his delight in troops of friends, in large hospitality, in cheerful giving. Let Timon,[118] let Warwick,[119] let Antonio the merchant[120] answer for his great heart. So far from Shakspeare's being the least known, he is the one person, in all modern history, known to us. What point of morals, of manners, of economy, of philosophy, of religion, of taste, of the conduct of life, has he not settled? What mystery has he not signified his knowledge of? What office, or function, or district

---

115. John Aubrey (1626–1697), an English historian.
116. Nicholas Rowe (1674–1718), an English writer and biographer of Shakespeare.
117. Pronounced uh-KUHLT. Here, means secret.
118. A character in Shakespeare's *Timon of Athens*.
119. Richard Neville, 16th Earl of Warwick (1428–1471), an extremely wealthy and powerful English politician, sometimes referred to as "Warsick the Kingmaker." He appears in several of Shakepeare's Henries.
120. From Shakespeare's *Merchant of Venice*.

of man's work, has he not remembered? What king has he not taught state, as Talma[121] taught Napoleon? What maiden has not found him finer than her delicacy? What lover has he not outloved? What sage has he not outseen? What gentleman has he not instructed in the rudeness of his behavior?

Some able and appreciating critics think no criticism on Shakspeare valuable that does not rest purely on the dramatic merit; that he is falsely judged as poet and philosopher. I think as highly as these critics of his dramatic merit, but still think it secondary. He was a full man, who liked to talk; a brain exhaling thoughts and images, which, seeking vent, found the drama next at hand. Had he been less, we should have had to consider how well he filled his place, how good a dramatist he was,—and he is the best in the world. But it turns out that what he has to say is of that weight as to withdraw some attention from the vehicle; and he is like some saint whose history is to be rendered into all languages, into verse and prose, into songs and pictures, and cut up into proverbs; so that the occasion which gave the saint's meaning the form of a conversation, or of a prayer, or of a code of laws, is immaterial compared with the universality of its application. So it fares with the wise Shakspeare and his book of life. He wrote the airs for all our modern music: he wrote the text of modern life; the text of manners: he drew the man of England and Europe; the father of the man in America; he drew the man, and described the day, and what is done in it: he read the hearts of men and women, their probity,[122] and their second thought and wiles; the wiles of innocence, and the transitions by which virtues and vices slide into their contraries: he could divide the mother's part from the father's part in the face of the child, or draw the fine demarcations of freedom and of fate: he knew the laws of repression which make the police of nature: and all the sweets and all the terrors of human lot lay in his mind as truly

---

121. A French actor Napoleon enjoyed.
122. Pronounced PROE-buh-tee. Righteousness.

but as softly as the landscape lies on the eye. And the importance of this wisdom of life sinks the form, as of Drama or Epic, out of notice. 'Tis like making a question concerning the paper on which a king's message is written.

21 Shakspeare is as much out of the category of eminent authors, as he is out of the crowd. He is inconceivably wise; the others, conceivably. A good reader can, in a sort, nestle into Plato's[123] brain and think from thence; but not into Shakspeare's. We are still out of doors. For executive faculty, for creation, Shakspeare is unique. No man can imagine it better. He was the farthest reach of subtlety compatible with an individual self,— the subtilest of authors, and only just within the possibility of authorship. With this wisdom of life is the equal endowment of imaginative and of lyric power. He clothed the creatures of his legend with form and sentiments as if they were people who had lived under his roof; and few real men have left such distinct characters as these fictions. And they spoke in language as sweet as it was fit. Yet his talents never seduced him into an ostentation, nor did he harp on one string. An omnipresent humanity co-ordinates all his faculties. Give a man of talents a story to tell, and his partiality will presently appear. He has certain observations, opinions, topics, which have some accidental prominence, and which he disposes all to exhibit. He crams this part and starves that other part, consulting not the fitness of the thing, but his fitness and strength. But Shakspeare has no peculiarity, no importunate[124] topic; but all is duly given; no veins, no curiosities; no cow-painter, no bird-fancier,[125] no mannerist[126] is he:

---

123. See Plato footnote on page 8.
124. Pronounced ihm-POR-chuh-nent. Urgent.
125. Emerson may have been referring to the widespread use of cows in nineteenth-century landscape paintings to represent hard work and rural life. "Bird fancier" may refer to a trend of bird watching made famous by John James Audubon's (1785–1851) book *Birds of America*.
126. Mannerism was a style of art from the late Renaissance that exaggerated the qualities of its subjects. The painter El Greco is a good example.

he has no discoverable egotism: the great he tells greatly; the small subordinately. He is wise without emphasis or assertion; he is strong, as nature is strong, who lifts the land into mountain slopes without effort and by the same rule as she floats a bubble in the air, and likes as well to do the one as the other. This makes that equality of power in farce, tragedy, narrative, and love-songs; a merit so incessant that each reader is incredulous of the perception of other readers.

This power of expression, or of transferring the inmost truth of things into music and verse, makes him the type of the poet and has added a new problem to metaphysics. This is that which throws him into natural history, as a main production of the globe, and as announcing new eras and ameliorations. Things were mirrored in his poetry without loss or blur: he could paint the fine with precision, the great with compass, the tragic and the comic indifferently and without any distortion or favor. He carried his powerful execution into minute details, to a hair point; finishes an eyelash or a dimple as firmly as he draws a mountain; and yet these, like nature's, will bear the scrutiny of the solar microscope.

In short, he is the chief example to prove that more or less of production, more or fewer pictures, is a thing indifferent. He had the power to make one picture. Daguerre[127] learned how to let one flower etch its image on his plate of iodine,[128] and then proceeds at leisure to etch a million. There are always objects; but there was never representation. Here is perfect representation, at last; and now let the world of figures sit for their portraits. No recipe can be given for the making of a Shakspeare; but the possibility of the translation of things into song is demonstrated.

His lyric power lies in the genius of the piece. The sonnets, though their excellence is lost in the splendor of the dramas, are

---
127. Louis Daguerre (1787–1851), a French artist and photographer.
128. Silver iodine is sensitive to light and was used in the process of creating the first photographic plates.

as inimitable[129] as they; and it is not a merit of lines, but a total merit of the piece; like the tone of voice of some incomparable person, so is this a speech of poetic beings, and any clause as unproducible now as a whole poem.

Though the speeches in the plays, and single lines, have a beauty which tempts the ear to pause on them for their euphuism,[130] yet the sentence is so loaded with meaning and so linked with its foregoers and followers, that the logician is satisfied. His means are as admirable as his ends; every subordinate invention, by which he helps himself to connect some irreconcilable opposites, is a poem too. He is not reduced to dismount and walk because his horses are running off with him in some distant direction: he always rides.

The finest poetry was first experience; but the thought has suffered a transformation since it was an experience. Cultivated men often attain a good degree of skill in writing verses; but it is easy to read, through their poems, their personal history: any one acquainted with the parties can name every figure; this is Andrew and that is Rachel.[131] The sense thus remains prosaic[132]. It is a caterpillar with wings, and not yet a butterfly. In the poet's mind the fact has gone quite over into the new element of thought, and has lost all that is exuvial[133]. This generosity abides with Shakespeare. We say, from the truth and closeness of his pictures, that he knows the lesson by heart. Yet there is not a trace of egotism.

One more royal trait properly belongs to the poet. I mean his cheerfulness, without which no man can be a poet,—for beauty is his aim. He loves virtue, not for its obligation but for

---

129. Pronounced ih-NIHM-ih-tuh-bull. Impossible to imitate.
130. Pronounced YOO-fyoo-ih-zuhm. Contrived linguistic elegance.
131. President Andrew Jackson (1767–1845) and his wife, Rachel (1767–1828).
132. Pronounced proe-ZAY-ihk. Unpoetic, uninspired. (Remember the definition of "prose.")
133. Pronounced ihg-ZOO-vee-uhl. Pertaining to an outer shell or skin.

its grace: he delights in the world, in man, in woman, for the lovely light that sparkles from them. Beauty, the spirit of joy and hilarity, he sheds over the universe. Epicurus[134] relates that poetry hath such charms that a lover might forsake his mistress to partake of them. And the true bards have been noted for their firm and cheerful temper. Homer lies in sunshine; Chaucer is glad and erect; and Saadi says, "It was rumored abroad that I was penitent[135]; but what had I to do with repentance?" Not less sovereign and cheerful,—much more sovereign and cheerful, is the tone of Shakespeare. His name suggests joy and emancipation to the heart of men. If he should appear in any company of human souls, who would not march in his troop? He touches nothing that does not borrow health and longevity from his festal[136] style.

28

AND NOW, HOW STANDS THE ACCOUNT OF MAN WITH THIS BARD and benefactor, when, in solitude, shutting our ears to the reverberations of his fame, we seek to strike the balance? Solitude has austere[137] lessons; it can teach us to spare both heroes and poets; and it weighs Shakespeare also, and finds him to share the halfness and imperfection of humanity.

29

Shakespeare, Homer, Dante, Chaucer, saw the splendor of meaning that plays over the visible world; knew that a tree had another use than for apples, and corn another than for meal, and the ball of the earth, than for tillage and roads: that these things bore a second and finer harvest to the mind, being emblems of its thoughts, and conveying in all their natural history a certain mute commentary on human life. Shakespeare employed them as colors to compose his picture. He rested in their beauty; and

---

134. Epicurus (341–270 BC), the Greek philosopher who founded Epicureanism, the belief that happiness is the highest good.
135. Pronounced PEHN-ih-tehnt. Humbly repentant.
136. Pronounced FEST-uhl. Celebratory.
137. Pronounced ah/aw-STAYR. Here, means severe or harsh.

never took the step which seemed inevitable to such genius, namely to explore the virtue which resides in these symbols and imparts this power:—what is that which they themselves say? He converted the elements which waited on his command, into entertainments. He was master of the revels to mankind. Is it not as if one should have, through majestic powers of science, the comets given into his hand, or the planets and their moons, and should draw them from their orbits to glare with the municipal fireworks on a holiday night, and advertise in all towns, "Very superior pyrotechny[138] this evening"? Are the agents of nature, and the power to understand them, worth no more than a street serenade, or the breath of a cigar? One remembers again the trumpet-text in the Koran,—"The heavens and the earth and all that is between them, think ye we have created them in jest?"[139] As long as the question is of talent and mental power, the world of men has not his equal to show. But when the question is, to life and its materials and its auxiliaries,[140] how does he profit me? What does it signify? It is but a *Twelfth Night*, or *Midsummer-Night's Dream*, or *Winter Evening's Tale*: what signifies another picture more or less? The Egyptian verdict of the Shakespeare Societies comes to mind; that he was a jovial actor and manager. I can not marry this fact to his verse. Other admirable men have led lives in some sort of keeping with their thought; but this man, in wide contrast. Had he been less, had he reached only the common measure of great authors, of Bacon, Milton, Tasso,[141] Cervantes,[142] we might leave the fact in the twilight of human fate: but that this man of men, he who gave to the science of mind a new and larger subject than had ever existed, and

---

138. Pronounced pie-roe-TEHK-nee. Technology concerning fire.
139. From Surah Ad-Dukhan 44:38..
140. Pronounced aug-ZIHL-yuh-reez. Pieces of equipment; useful tools.
141. Torquato Tasso (1544–1595), an Italian poet famous for his epic poem *Gerusalemme Liberata* (*Jerusalem Delivered*) about the Crusades.
142. Miguel de Cervantes (1547–1616), a Spanish writer who wrote *Don Quixote*, an adventure story of a man who wants to be great but lacks some key virtues.

planted the standard of humanity some furlongs[143] forward into Chaos,—that he should not be wise for himself;—it must even go into the world's history that the best poet led an obscure and profane life, using his genius for the public amusement.

Well, other men, priest and prophet, Israelite, German and Swede, beheld the same objects: they also saw through them that which was contained. And to what purpose? The beauty straightway vanished; they read commandments, all-excluding mountainous duty; an obligation, a sadness, as of piled mountains, fell on them, and life became ghastly, joyless, a pilgrim's progress, a probation, beleaguered[144] round with doleful histories of Adam's fall and curse behind us; with doomsdays and purgatorial[145] and penal[146] fires before us; and the heart of the seer and the heart of the listener sank in them.

It must be conceded that these are half-views of half-men. The world still wants its poet-priest, a reconciler, who shall not trifle, with Shakespeare the player, nor shall grope in graves, with Swedenborg the mourner; but who shall see, speak, and act, with equal inspiration. For knowledge will brighten the sunshine; right is more beautiful than private affection; and love is compatible with universal wisdom.

---

143. Pronounced FER-longz. A furlong is 220 yards.
144. Pronounced b'LEE-ger'd. Surrounded, in the context of battle.
145. Pronounced per-guh-TOR-ee-uhl. Having to do with purgatory. Some people, particularly Catholics, believe that there is a place between heaven and hell in the afterlife where one suffers until penance for minor sins is paid, and the soul is able to "get into" Heaven. This place is called purgatory.
146. Pronounced PEE-nuhl. Of punishment.

ABOVE: Walden Pond from *Haunts of Emerson*, illustrated by Louis K. Harlow, published 1889.
LEFT: Lithograph of R. W. Emerson, 1859.

— **1856** *publishes English Traits*

— **1858** *holds* two-week "Philosophers Camp" at Follensbee Pond, New York

— **1856** *publishes The Conduct of Life*

— **1862** *Thoreau dies* May 6

"Thoreau gives me in flesh & blood & pertinacious Saxon belief, my own ethics. He is far more real, & daily practicing obeying them, than I; and fortifies my memory at all times with an affirmative experience which refuses to be set aside."
—Emerson, journal entry

— **1862** *publishes* "Thoreau" in *The Atlantic Monthly* (August)

THOREAU

A QUEEN rejoices in her peers,
And wary Nature knows her own,
By court and city, dale and down,
And like a lover volunteers,
And to her son will treasures more,
And more to purpose, freely pour
In one wood walk, than learned men
Will find with glass in ten times ten.[1]

IT seemed as if the breezes brought him,
It seemed as if the sparrows taught him,
As if by secret sign he knew
Where in far fields the orchis grew.[2]

1

HENRY DAVID THOREAU was the last male descendant of a French ancestor who came to this country from the Isle of Guernsey. His character exhibited occasional traits drawn from this blood, in singular combination with a very strong Saxon genius.

---

1. From "The Walk" by Emerson.
2. From "Woody Notes" by Emerson.

2   He was born in Concord, Massachusetts, on the 12th of July, 1817. He was graduated at Harvard College in 1837, but without any literary distinction. An iconoclast[3] in literature, he seldom thanked colleges for their service to him, holding them in small esteem, whilst yet his debt to them was important. After leaving the University, he joined his brother in teaching a private school, which he soon renounced. His father was a manufacturer of lead-pencils, and Henry applied himself for a time to this craft, believing he could make a better pencil than was then in use. After completing his experiments, he exhibited his work to chemists and artists in Boston, and having obtained their certificates to its excellence and to its equality with the best London manufacture, he returned home contented. His friends congratulated him that he had now opened his way to fortune. But he replied that he should never make another pencil. "Why should I? I would not do again what I have done once." He resumed his endless walks and miscellaneous studies, making every day some new acquaintance with Nature, though as yet never speaking of zoölogy[4] or botany, since, though very studious of natural facts, he was incurious[5] of technical and textual science.

3   At this time, a strong, healthy youth, fresh from college, whilst all his companions were choosing their profession, or eager to begin some lucrative employment, it was inevitable that his thoughts should be exercised on the same question, and it required rare decision to refuse all the accustomed paths and keep his solitary freedom at the cost of disappointing the natural expectations of his family and friends: all the more difficult that he had a perfect probity, was exact in securing his own independence, and in holding every man to the like duty. But Thoreau never faltered. He was a born protestant. He declined to give up

---

3. Pronounced eye-KAHN-oe-klast. Someone who disapproves of symbols or icons.

4. Pronounced zoe-AH-luh-jee. The scientific study of animals.

5. Pronounced in-KYER-ee-uss. Not curious.

his large ambition of knowledge and action for any narrow craft or profession, aiming at a much more comprehensive calling, the art of living well. If he slighted and defied the opinions of others, it was only that he was more intent to reconcile his practice with his own belief. Never idle or self-indulgent, he preferred, when he wanted money, earning it by some piece of manual labor agreeable to him, as building a boat or a fence, planting, grafting,[6] surveying or other short work, to any long engagements. With his hardy habits and few wants, his skill in wood-craft, and his powerful arithmetic, he was very competent to live in any part of the world. It would cost him less time to supply his wants than another. He was therefore secure of his leisure.

A natural skill for mensuration,[7] growing out of his mathematical knowledge and his habit of ascertaining the measures and distances of objects which interested him, the size of trees, the depth and extent of ponds and rivers, the height of mountains and the air-line distance of his favorite summits,— this, and his intimate knowledge of the territory about Concord, made him drift into the profession of land-surveyor. It had the advantage for him that it led him continually into new and secluded grounds, and helped his studies of Nature. His accuracy and skill in this work were readily appreciated, and he found all the employment he wanted.

He could easily solve the problems of the surveyor, but he was daily beset with graver questions, which he manfully confronted. He interrogated every custom, and wished to settle all his practice on an ideal foundation. He was a protestant *à outrance*,[8] and few lives contain so many renunciations. He was

---

6. Pronounced GRAF-teeng. Grafting is a process by which a limb from one tree is cut off and attached to the site of a severed limb from another tree. The new limb should grow to become a part of the larger tree. The idea is that by grafting, one could create a tree that grows both apples and oranges by attaching a severed apple tree branch onto where an orange tree branch formerly grew.

7. Pronounced mehn-ser-AY-shun. Measuring.

8. French, meaning "to excess."

bred to no profession; he never married; he lived alone; he never went to church; he never voted; he refused to pay a tax to the State; he ate no flesh, he drank no wine, he never knew the use of tobacco; and, though a naturalist, he used neither trap nor gun. He chose, wisely no doubt for himself, to be the bachelor of thought and Nature. He had no talent for wealth, and knew how to be poor without the least hint of squalor or inelegance. Perhaps he fell into his way of living without forecasting it much, but approved it with later wisdom. "I am often reminded," he wrote in his journal, "that if I had bestowed on me the wealth of Crœsus,[9] my aims must be still the same, and my means essentially the same." He had no temptations, to fight against,—no appetites, no passions, no taste for elegant trifles. A fine house, dress, the manners and talk of highly cultivated people were all thrown away on him. He much preferred a good Indian,[10] and considered these refinements as impediments to conversation, wishing to meet his companion on the simplest terms. He declined invitations to dinner-parties, because there each was in every one's way, and he could not meet the individuals to any purpose. "They make their pride," he said, "in making their dinner cost much; I make my pride in making my dinner cost little." When asked at table what dish he preferred, he answered, "The nearest." He did not like the taste of wine, and never had a vice in his life. He said,—"I have a faint recollection of pleasure derived from smoking dried lily-stems, before I was a man. I had commonly a supply of these. I have never smoked anything more noxious."

---

9. Croesus (c. 595–546 BC), a Greek king of Lydia (now in Turkey) who was famous for his wealth.
10. Readers will find Emerson (and Thoreau) thought-provoking for different reasons: some positive, some negative. Unfortunately, Emerson subscribed to some of his day's misguided opinions about Native Americans. His references to "savages" should be met, first, with regret that such views lingered and, second, with a fresh commitment to honor all who are made in God's image.

6 He chose to be rich by making his wants few, and supplying them himself. In his travels, he used the railroad only to get over so much country as was unimportant to the present purpose, walking hundred of miles, avoiding taverns, buying a lodging in farmers' and fishermen's houses, as cheaper, and more agreeable to him, and because there he could better find the men and the information he wanted.

7 There was somewhat military in his nature, not to be subdued, always manly and able, but rarely tender, as if he did not feel himself except in opposition. He wanted a fallacy to expose, a blunder to pillory,[11] I may say required a little sense of victory, a roll of the drum, to call his powers into full exercise. It cost him nothing to say No; indeed he found it much easier than to say Yes. It seemed as if his first instinct on hearing a proposition was to controvert[12] it, so impatient was he of the limitations of our daily thought. This habit, of course, is a little chilling to the social affections; and though the companion would in the end acquit him of any malice or untruth, yet it mars conversation. Hence, no equal companion stood in affectionate relations with one so pure and guileless. "I love Henry," said one of his friends,[13] "but I cannot like him; and as for taking his arm, I should as soon think of taking the arm of an elm-tree."

8 Yet, hermit and stoic as he was, he was really fond of sympathy, and threw himself heartily and childlike into the company of young people whom he loved, and whom he delighted to entertain, as he only could, with the varied and endless anecdotes of his experiences by field and river: and he was always ready to lead a huckleberry-party or a search for chestnuts or grapes. Talking, one day, of a public discourse, Henry remarked that whatever succeeded with the audience

---

11. Pronounced PIHL-er-ee. A synonym for the stocks. Basically Thoreau loved to put things on show for the purpose of their being made fun of.
12. Pronounced kahn-truh-VERT. Contradict.
13. From Emerson's journal, dated August 1848.

was bad. I said, "Who would not like to write something which all can read, like *Robinson Crusoe*[14]? and who does not see with regret that his page is not solid with a right materialistic treatment, which delights everybody?" Henry objected, of course, and vaunted[15] the better lectures which reached only a few persons. But, at supper, a young girl, understanding that he was to lecture at the Lyceum,[16] sharply asked him, "Whether his lecture would be a nice, interesting story, such as she wished to hear, or whether it was one of those old philosophical things that she did not care about." Henry turned to her, and bethought himself, and, I saw, was trying to believe that he had matter that might fit her and her brother, who were to sit up and go to the lecture, if it was a good one for them.

9

He was a speaker and actor of the truth, born such, and was ever running into dramatic situations from this cause. In any circumstance it interested all bystanders to know what part Henry would take, and what he would say; and he did not disappoint expectation, but used an original judgment on each emergency. In 1845 he built himself a small framed house on the shores of Walden Pond, and lived there two years alone, a life of labor and study.[17] This action was quite native and fit for him. No one who knew him would tax him with affectation[18]. He was more unlike his neighbors in his thought than in his action. As soon as he had exhausted the advantages of that solitude, he abandoned it. In 1847, not approving some uses to which the public expenditure was applied,[19] he refused to pay his town tax,

---

14. Published in 1719, *Robinson Crusoe* by Daniel Defoe is sometimes considered the first novel.
15. Pronounced VAHNT-ehd. Boasted of.
16. Pronounced lye-SEE-um. Named for a gymnasium and gathering place in Athens, the lyceum movement in the United States gathered speakers and entertainers for adult education, mainly before the Civil War.
17. You can read all about this in Thoreau's *Walden, or Life in the Woods*.
18. Pronounced a-fehk-TAY-shun. False pretense; an artificial show.
19. Referring to spending on the Mexican-American War.

and was put in jail. A friend paid the tax for him,[20] and he was released. The like annoyance was threatened the next year. But as his friends paid the tax, notwithstanding his protest, I believe he ceased to resist. No opposition or ridicule had any weight with him. He coldly and fully stated his opinion without affecting[21] to believe that it was the opinion of the company. It was of no consequence if every one present held the opposite opinion. On one occasion he went to the University Library to procure some books. The librarian refused to lend them. Mr. Thoreau repaired to the President,[22] who stated to him the rules and usages, which permitted the loan of books to resident graduates, to clergymen who were alumni, and to some others resident within a circle of ten miles' radius from the College. Mr. Thoreau explained to the President that the railroad had destroyed the old scale of distances,—that the library was useless, yes, and President and College useless, on the terms of his rules,—that the one benefit he owed to the College was its library,—that, at this moment, not only his want of books was imperative, but he wanted a large number of books, and assured him that he, Thoreau, and not the librarian, was the proper custodian of these. In short, the President found the petitioner so formidable, and the rules getting to look so ridiculous, that he ended by giving him a privilege which in his hands proved unlimited thereafter.

10 No truer American existed than Thoreau. His preference of his country and condition was genuine, and his aversation from English and European manners and tastes almost reached contempt. He listened impatiently to news or *bonmots*[23] gleaned from London circles; and though he tried to be civil, these

---

20. Likely Thoreau's aunt, Marie Thoreau (1794–1881) or Elizabeth Hoar (1814–1878), fiancee of Emerson's brother Charles (Charles died of consumption before the wedding) and a schoolmate of Thoreau.
21. Pretending.
22. President of the university.
23. Pronounced baun-MWAZ. Witty anecdotes.

anecdotes fatigued him. The men were all imitating each other, and on a small mould. Why can they not live as far apart as possible, and each be a man by himself? What he sought was the most energetic nature; and he wished to go to Oregon, not to London. "In every part of Great Britain," he wrote in his diary, "are discovered traces of the Romans, their funereal urns, their camps, their roads, their dwellings. But New England, at least, is not based on any Roman ruins. We have not to lay the foundations of our houses on the ashes of a former civilization."

11 But idealist as he was, standing for abolition of slavery, abolition of tariffs,[24] almost for abolition of government, it is needless to say he found himself not only unrepresented in actual politics, but almost equally opposed to every class of reformers. Yet he paid the tribute of his uniform respect to the Anti-Slavery party[25]. One man, whose personal acquaintance he had formed, he honored with exceptional regard. Before the first friendly word had been spoken for Captain John Brown,[26] he sent notices to most houses in Concord that he would speak in a public hall on the condition and character of John Brown, on Sunday evening, and invited all people to come. The Republican Committee, the Abolitionist Committee, sent him word that it was premature and not advisable. He replied,—"I did not send to you for advice, but to announce that I am to speak." The hall was filled at an early hour by people of all parties, and his earnest eulogy of the hero was heard by all respectfully, by many with a sympathy that surprised themselves.

12 It was said of Plotinus[27] that he was ashamed of his body, and 't is very likely he had good reason for it,—that his body was

---

24. Pronounced TEHR-ifs. Taxes on imported and/or exported goods.
25. The political views held by the Anti-Slavery Society, with which Frederick Douglass was involved.
26. Brown (1800–1859), an American abolitionist who believed in violent opposition to slavery. He unsuccessfully attempted to incite a slave revolt in 1859, and was subsequently hanged for treason.
27. Plotinus (203–270), a Greek philosopher influenced by Plato.

a bad servant, and he had not skill in dealing with the material world, as happens often to men of abstract intellect. But Mr. Thoreau was equipped with a most adapted and serviceable body. He was of short stature, firmly built, of light complexion, with strong, serious blue eyes, and a grave aspect,—his face covered in the late years with a becoming beard. His senses were acute, his frame well-knit and hardy, his hands strong and skilful in the use of tools. And there was a wonderful fitness of body and mind. He could pace sixteen rods[28] more accurately than another man could measure them with rod and chain. He could find his path in the woods at night, he said, better by his feet than his eyes. He could estimate the measure of a tree very well by his eye; he could estimate the weight of a calf or a pig, like a dealer. From a box containing a bushel or more of loose pencils, he could take up with his hands fast enough just a dozen pencils at every grasp. He was a good swimmer, runner, skater, boatman, and would probably outwalk most countrymen in a day's journey. And the relation of body to mind was still finer than we have indicated. He said he wanted every stride his legs made. The length of his walk uniformly made the length of his writing. If shut up in the house he did not write at all.

He had a strong common sense, like that which Rose Flammock, the weaver's daughter in Scott's romance,[29] commends in her father, as resembling a yardstick, which, whilst it measures dowlas[30] and diaper, can equally well measure tapestry and cloth of gold. He had always a new resource. When I was planting forest trees, and had procured half a peck of acorns, he said that only a small portion of them would be sound, and proceeded to examine them and select the sound ones. But finding this took time, he said, "I think if you put them all into water the good ones will sink;" which experiment

---

28. A rod is a surveyor's tool, measuring sixteen and one-half feet.
29. *The Betrothed*, written by Sir Walter Scott (1771–1832) and published in 1825.
30. Pronounced DOW-luhs. (*DOW* rhymes with "cow.") A thin, rough cloth.

we tried with success. He could plan a garden or a house or a barn; would have been competent to lead a "Pacific Exploring Expedition[31];" could give judicious counsel in the gravest private or public affairs.

He lived for the day, not cumbered and mortified by his memory. If he brought you yesterday a new proposition, he would bring you to-day another not less revolutionary. A very industrious man, and setting, like all highly organized men, a high value on his time, he seemed the only man of leisure in town, always ready for any excursion that promised well, or for conversation prolonged into late hours. His trenchant[32] sense was never stopped by his rules of daily prudence, but was always up to the new occasion. He liked and used the simplest food, yet, when some one urged a vegetable diet, Thoreau thought all diets a very small matter, saying that "the man who shoots the buffalo lives better than the man who boards at the Graham House[33]." He said,—"You can sleep near the railroad, and never be disturbed: Nature knows very well what sounds are worth attending to, and has made up her mind not to hear the railroad-whistle. But things respect the devout mind, and a mental ecstasy was never interrupted." He noted what repeatedly befell him, that, after receiving from a distance a rare plant, he would presently find the same in his own haunts. And those pieces of luck which happen only to good players happened to him. One day, walking with a stranger, who inquired where Indian arrow-heads could be found, he replied, "Everywhere," and, stooping forward, picked one on the instant from the ground. At Mount Washington, in Tuckerman's Ravine, Thoreau had a bad fall, and

---

31. An expedition (1853–1856) organized by the United States navy to survey the north Pacific seas, the Bering Strait, and the coasts of Japan and China.
32. Pronounced TREHN-chunt. Keen, sharp.
33. Graham House was built in southern West Virginia around 1770. In 1777, a famous Indian attack occurred here.

sprained his foot. As he was in the act of getting up from his fall, he saw for the first time the leaves of the *Arnica mollis*[34].

15 His robust common sense, armed with stout hands, keen perceptions and strong will, cannot yet account for the superiority which shone in his simple and hidden life. I must add the cardinal fact, that there was an excellent wisdom in him, proper to a rare class of men, which showed him the material world as a means and symbol. This discovery, which sometimes yields to poets a certain casual and interrupted light, serving for the ornament of their writing, was in him an unsleeping insight; and whatever faults or obstructions of temperament might cloud it, he was not disobedient to the heavenly vision. In his youth, he said, one day, "The other world is all my art; my pencils will draw no other; my jack-knife will cut nothing else; I do not use it as a means." This was the muse and genius that ruled his opinions, conversation, studies, work and course of life. This made him a searching judge of men. At first glance he measured his companion, and, though insensible to some fine traits of culture, could very well report his weight and calibre[35]. And this made the impression of genius which his conversation sometimes gave.

16 He understood the matter in hand at a glance, and saw the limitations and poverty of those he talked with, so that nothing seemed concealed from such terrible eyes. I have repeatedly known young men of sensibility converted in a moment to the belief that this was the man they were in search of, the man of men, who could tell them all they should do. His own dealing with them was never affectionate, but superior, didactic,[36] scorning their petty ways,—very slowly conceding, or not conceding at all, the promise of his society at their houses, or even at his own. "Would he not walk with them?" "He did not

---
34. A relative of the sunflower.
35. Pronounced KAL-ih-ber. Degree of quality, character.
36. Pronounced die-DAK-tihc. Intended to teach.

know. There was nothing so important to him as his walk; he had no walks to throw away on company." Visits were offered him from respectful parties, but he declined them. Admiring friends offered to carry him at their own cost to the Yellowstone River,—to the West Indies,—to South America. But though nothing could be more grave or considered than his refusals, they remind one, in quite new relations, of that fop Brummel's[37] reply to the gentleman who offered him his carriage in a shower, "But where will you ride, then?"—and what accusing silences, and what searching and irresistible speeches, battering down all defences, his companions can remember!

17   Mr. Thoreau dedicated his genius with such entire love to the fields, hills and waters of his native town, that he made them known and interesting to all reading Americans, and to people over the sea. The river on whose banks he was born and died he knew from its springs to its confluence[38] with the Merrimack[39]. He had made summer and winter observations on it for many years, and at every hour of the day and night. The result of the recent survey of the Water Commissioners appointed by the State of Massachusetts he had reached by his private experiments, several years earlier. Every fact which occurs in the bed, on the banks or in the air over it; the fishes, and their spawning and nests, their manners, their food; the shad-flies[40] which fill the air on a certain evening once a year, and which are snapped at by the fishes so ravenously that many of these die of repletion; the conical heaps of small stones on the river-shallows, the huge nests of small fishes, one of which will sometimes overfill a cart; the birds which frequent the stream, heron, duck, sheldrake,

---

37. Beau Brummell (1778–1840), an Englishman known for his wit and love for fashion.
38. Pronounced KAHN-floo-ents or kuhn-FLOO-ents. Things are confluent if they come or flow together.
39. A river in northeastern United States
40. Also called a mayfly; an aquatic insect with wings that stand up like a butterfly's when it lands, and has a long tail consisting of two thin pieces.

drake, loon, osprey; the snake, muskrat, otter, woodchuck and fox, on the banks; the turtle, frog, hyla and cricket, which make the banks vocal,—were all known to him, and, as it were, townsmen and fellow creatures; so that he felt an absurdity or violence in any narrative of one of these by itself apart, and still more of its dimensions on an inch-rule, or in the exhibition of its skeleton, or the specimen of a squirrel or a bird in brandy. He liked to speak of the manners of the river, as itself a lawful creature, yet with exactness, and always to an observed fact. As he knew the river, so the ponds in this region.

18 One of the weapons he used, more important to him than microscope or alcohol-receiver to other investigators, was a whim which grew on him by indulgence, yet appeared in gravest statement, namely, of extolling[41] his own town and neighborhood as the most favored centre for natural observation. He remarked that the Flora[42] of Massachusetts embraced almost all the important plants of America,—most of the oaks, most of the willows, the best pines, the ash, the maple, the beech, the nuts. He returned Kane's Arctic Voyage[43] to a friend of whom he had borrowed it, with the remark, that "Most of the phenomena noted might be observed in Concord." He seemed a little envious of the Pole, for the coincident[44] sunrise and sunset, or five minutes' day after six months: a splendid fact, which Annursnuc[45] had never afforded him. He found red snow[46] in one of his walks, and told me that he expected to

---

41. Pronounced ehk-STOLE-eeng. Praising.
42. Plant life (as opposed to fauna, animal life).
43. *Arctic Explorations*, published by Elisha Kent Kane (1820–1857) in 1857. The work is a two-volume piece documenting his journey.
44. Pronounced coe-in-SIHN-dent. Things are coincident if they occur together or at the same time.
45. A hill near Concord.
46. Mentioned in Thoreau's journal, January 21, 1853: "Saw one faint tinge of red on red ice pond-hole, six inches over."

find yet the *Victoria regia*[47] in Concord. He was the attorney of the indigenous plants, and owned to a preference of the weeds to the imported plants, as of the Indian to the civilized man, and noticed, with pleasure, that the willow bean-poles of his neighbor had grown more than his beans. "See these weeds," he said, "which have been hoed at by a million farmers all spring and summer, and yet have prevailed, and just now come out triumphant over all lanes, pastures, fields and gardens, such is their vigor. We have insulted them with low names, too,—as Pigweed, Wormwood, Chickweed, Shad-blossom." He says, "They have brave names, too,—Ambrosia, Stellaria, Amelanchier, Amaranth, etc."

19 I think his fancy for referring everything to the meridian of Concord[48] did not grow out of any ignorance or depreciation of other longitudes or latitudes, but was rather a playful expression of his conviction of the indifferency of all places, and that the best place for each is where he stands. He expressed it once in this wise: "I think nothing is to be hoped from you, if this bit of mould[49] under your feet is not sweeter to you to eat than any other in this world, or in any world."

20 The other weapon with which he conquered all obstacles in science was patience. He knew how to sit immovable, a part of the rock he rested on, until the bird, the reptile, the fish, which had retired from him, should come back and resume its habits, nay, moved by curiosity, should come to him and watch him.

21 It was a pleasure and a privilege to walk with him. He knew the country like a fox or a bird, and passed through it as freely by paths of his own. He knew every track in the snow or on the ground, and what creature had taken this path before him. One must submit abjectly[50] to such a guide, and the reward

---

47. A relative of the water lily.
48. That is., acting like Concord is the center of the world.
49. Sounds like "mold." Soil, earth.
50. Pronounced ab-JEKT-lee. In a lowly, submissive manner.

was great. Under his arm he carried an old music-book to press plants[51]; in his pocket, his diary and pencil, a spy-glass for birds, microscope, jack-knife and twine. He wore a straw hat, stout shoes, strong gray trousers, to brave scrub-oaks and smilax,[52] and to climb a tree for a hawk's or a squirrel's nest. He waded into the pool for the water-plants, and his strong legs were no insignificant part of his armor. On the day I speak of he looked for the Menyanthes,[53] detected it across the wide pool, and, on examination of the florets,[54] decided that it had been in flower five days. He drew out of his breast-pocket his diary, and read the names of all the plants that should bloom on this day, whereof he kept account as a banker when his notes fall due. The Cypripedium[55] not due till to-morrow. He thought that, if waked up from a trance, in this swamp, he could tell by the plants what time of the year it was within two days. The redstart[56] was flying about, and presently the fine grosbeaks, whose brilliant scarlet "makes the rash gazer wipe his eye,"[57] and whose fine clear note Thoreau compared to that of a tanager[58] which has got rid of its hoarseness. Presently he heard a note which he called that of the night-warbler, a bird he had never identified, had been in search of twelve years, which always, when he saw it, was in the act of diving down into a tree or bush, and which it was vain to seek; the only bird which sings indifferently by night and by day. I told him he must beware of finding and booking it, lest life should have nothing more to show him. He said, "What you

---

51. One can flatten and preserve flowers and other plants by putting them between the pages of a thick, heavy book for a while.
52. A thorny, woody plant with red berries.
53. An aquatic plant.
54. Pronounced FLOR-ehts. A small cluster of buds, or, here, small flowers.
55. A species of orchid, also known as lady's slipper.
56. A small black and orange bird.
57. From the poem "Vertue" (Virtue) by George Herbert (1593–1633).
58. Scarlet tanagers are a South American tropical bird that migrate to spend summers in New England. The male bird's raspy song sounds like "a robin with a sore throat."

seek in vain for, half your life, one day you come full upon, all the family at dinner. You seek it like a dream, and as soon as you find it you become its prey."

His interest in the flower or the bird lay very deep in his mind, was connected with Nature,—and the meaning of Nature was never attempted to be defined by him. He would not offer a memoir of his observations to the Natural History Society. "Why should I? To detach the description from its connections in my mind would make it no longer true or valuable to me: and they do not wish what belongs to it." His power of observation seemed to indicate additional senses. He saw as with microscope, heard as with ear-trumpet,[59] and his memory was a photographic[60] register of all he saw and heard. And yet none knew better than he that it is not the fact that imports, but the impression or effect of the fact on your mind. Every fact lay in glory in his mind, a type of the order and beauty of the whole.

His determination on Natural History was organic. He confessed that he sometimes felt like a hound or a panther, and, if born among Indians, would have been a fell hunter. But, restrained by his Massachusetts culture, he played out the game in this mild form of botany and ichthyology[61]. His intimacy with animals suggested what Thomas Fuller[62] records of Butler[63] the apiologist,[64] that "either he had told the bees things or the bees had told him." Snakes coiled round his legs; the fishes swam into his hand, and he took them out of the water; he pulled the

---

59. A funnel-shaped device used to direct sound waves into the ear of those who were hard of hearing. Beethoven used an ear-trumpet.
60. Photography was cutting-edge and developing quickly for scientific use.
61. Pronounced ihk-thee-AH-luh-jee. The study of fish. From the Greek *ichthus*, meaning "fish."
62. Fuller (c. 1608–1661), an English historian and clergyman, who wrote *History of the Worthies of England* and *A Pisgah-Sight of Palestine*, a historical geography of Jerusalem.
63. Charles Butler (1571–1647), an Englishman who wrote *The Feminine Monarchie*, a treatise on bees.
64. Pronounced ap-ee-AH-luh-jihst. A scientist who studies honey bees.

woodchuck out of its hole by the tail, and took the foxes under his protection from the hunters. Our naturalist had perfect magnanimity; he had no secrets: he would carry you to the heron's haunt, or even to his most prized botanical swamp,— possibly knowing that you could never find it again, yet willing to take his risks.

24 No college ever offered him a diploma, or a professor's chair; no academy made him its corresponding secretary, its discoverer or even its member. Perhaps these learned bodies feared the satire of his presence. Yet so much knowledge of Nature's secret and genius few others possessed; none in a more large and religious synthesis. For not a particle of respect had he to the opinions of any man or body of men, but homage solely to the truth itself; and as he discovered everywhere among doctors some leaning of courtesy, it discredited them. He grew to be revered and admired by his townsmen, who had at first known him only as an oddity. The farmers who employed him as a surveyor soon discovered his rare accuracy and skill, his knowledge of their lands, of trees, of birds, of Indian remains and the like, which enabled him to tell every farmer more than he knew before of his own farm; so that he began to feel a little as if Mr. Thoreau had better rights in his land than he. They felt, too, the superiority of character which addressed all men with a native authority.

25 Indian relics abound in Concord,—arrow-heads, stone chisels, pestles[65] and fragments of pottery; and on the riverbank, large heaps of clam-shells and ashes mark spots which the savages frequented. These, and every circumstance touching the Indian, were important in his eyes. His visits to Maine were chiefly for love of the Indian. He had the satisfaction of seeing the manufacture of the bark canoe, as well as of trying his hand in its management on the rapids. He was inquisitive about the

---

65. Pronounced PEH-stuhlz. Small club-like instruments used to grind a substance into powder.

making of the stone arrow-head, and in his last days charged a youth setting out for the Rocky Mountains to find an Indian who could tell him that: "It was well worth a visit to California to learn it." Occasionally, a small party of Penobscot Indians[66] would visit Concord, and pitch their tents for a few weeks in summer on the riverbank. He failed not to make acquaintance with the best of them; though he well knew that asking questions of Indians is like catechizing[67] beavers and rabbits. In his last visit to Maine he had great satisfaction from Joseph Polis,[68] an intelligent Indian of Oldtown, who was his guide for some weeks.

26 He was equally interested in every natural fact. The depth of his perception found likeness of law throughout Nature, and I know not any genius who so swiftly inferred universal law from the single fact. He was no pedant[69] of a department. His eye was open to beauty, and his ear to music. He found these, not in rare conditions, but wheresoever he went. He thought the best of music was in single strains; and he found poetic suggestion in the humming of the telegraph-wire.

27 His poetry might be bad or good; he no doubt wanted[70] a lyric facility and technical skill, but he had the source of poetry in his spiritual perception. He was a good reader and critic, and his judgment on poetry was to the ground of it. He could not be deceived as to the presence or absence of the poetic element in any composition, and his thirst for this made him negligent and perhaps scornful of superficial graces. He would pass by many delicate rhythms, but he would have detected every live stanza or line in a volume and knew very well where to find an equal poetic charm in prose. He was so enamoured of the spiritual

---

66. A Native American tribe in the northern United States and Canada.
67. Pronounced KAT-uh-kie-zeeng. (*Kie* rhymes with "pie.") Questioning systematically, or teaching by asking questions.
68. Thoreau describes his time with Polis in *The Maine Woods*.
69. Pronounced PEH-dent. A teacher, with the connotation of a dull or overbearing one.
70. Lacked.

beauty that he held all actual written poems in very light esteem in the comparison. He admired Æschylus[71] and Pindar[72]; but when some one was commending them, he said that Æschylus and the Greeks, in describing Apollo[73] and Orpheus,[74] had given no song, or no good one. "They ought not to have moved trees, but to have chanted to the gods such a hymn as would have sung all their old ideas out of their heads, and new ones in." His own verses are often rude and defective. The gold does not yet run pure, is drossy[75] and crude. The thyme and marjoram are not yet honey.[76] But if he want lyric fineness and technical merits, if he have not the poetic temperament, he never lacks the causal thought, showing that his genius was better than his talent. He knew the worth of the Imagination for the uplifting and consolation of human life, and liked to throw every thought into a symbol. The fact you tell is of no value, but only the impression. For this reason his presence was poetic, always piqued the curiosity to know more deeply the secrets of his mind. He had many reserves, an unwillingness to exhibit to profane eyes what was still sacred in his own, and knew well how to throw a poetic veil over his experience. All readers of *Walden* will remember his mythical record of his disappointments:—

28

"I long ago lost a hound, a bay horse and a turtle-dove, and am still on their trail. Many are the travellers I have spoken concerning them, describing their tracks, and what calls they answered to. I have met one or two who have heard the hound, and the tramp of the horse, and even seen the dove disappear

---

71. Pronounced EHS-kuh-luhss (c. 525–456 BC), an Athenian poet and one of her first dramatists.
72. Pindar (c. 522–443 BC), one of the Nine Lyric Poets of Greece.
73. The Greek god of the sun, but also music, poetry, and prophecy.
74. Pronounced OR-fee-uss. An amazing musician in Greek mythology, taught by Apollo.
75. Rhymes with "mossy." Dross is a useless film that forms on top of molten metal.
76. Some honey, especially in Greece, came from thyme or marjoram plants.

behind a cloud; and they seemed as anxious to recover them as if they had lost them themselves."

His riddles were worth the reading, and I confide that if at any time I do not understand the expression, it is yet just. Such was the wealth of his truth that it was not worth his while to use words in vain. His poem entitled "Sympathy" reveals the tenderness under that triple steel of stoicism, and the intellectual subtility it could animate. His classic poem on "Smoke" suggests Simonides,[77] but is better than any poem of Simonides. His biography is in his verses. His habitual thought makes all his poetry a hymn to the Cause of causes,[78] the Spirit which vivifies[79] and controls his own:—

> "I hearing get, who had but ears,
> And sight, who had but eyes before;
> I moments live, who lived but years,
> And truth discern, who knew but learning's lore."

And still more in these religious lines:—

> "Now chiefly is my natal hour,
> And only now my prime of life;
> I will not doubt the love untold,
> Which not my worth nor want have bought,
> Which wooed me young, and wooes me old,
> And to this evening hath me brought."[80]

Whilst he used in his writings a certain petulance of remark in reference to churches or churchmen, he was a person of a rare, tender and absolute religion, a person incapable of any profanation, by act or by thought. Of course, the same isolation which belonged to his original thinking and living detached him

---

77. Simonides (c. 556–468 BC), a Greek poet.
78. A reference to Aristotle's metaphysical theory of the four causes. Everything has four causes: a material (what is a thing made of?), an efficient (what created or caused it?), a formal (what is its structure), and a final (what is its purpose?).
79. Pronounced VIHV-ih-fize. Enlivens.
80. Excerpts from "Inspiration" by Thoreau.

from the social religious forms. This is neither to be censured nor regretted. Aristotle[81] long ago explained it, when he said, "One who surpasses his fellow citizens in virtue is no longer a part of the city. Their law is not for him, since he is a law to himself."[82]

32 Thoreau was sincerity itself, and might fortify the convictions of prophets in the ethical laws by his holy living. It was an affirmative experience which refused to be set aside. A truth-speaker he, capable of the most deep and strict conversation; a physician to the wounds of any soul; a friend, knowing not only the secret of friendship, but almost worshipped by those few persons who resorted to him as their confessor and prophet, and knew the deep value of his mind and great heart. He thought that without religion or devotion of some kind nothing great was ever accomplished: and he thought that the bigoted sectarian[83] had better bear this in mind.

33 His virtues, of course, sometimes ran into extremes. It was easy to trace to the inexorable[84] demand on all for exact truth that austerity which made this willing hermit more solitary even than he wished. Himself of a perfect probity, he required not less of others. He had a disgust at crime, and no worldly success would cover it. He detected paltering as readily in dignified and prosperous persons as in beggars, and with equal scorn. Such dangerous frankness was in his dealing that his admirers called him "that terrible Thoreau," as if he spoke when silent, and was still present when he had departed. I think the severity of his ideal interfered to deprive him of a healthy sufficiency of human society.

---

81. Aristotle (384–322 BC), a Greek philosopher who studied under Plato, but vastly differed in his beliefs. Where Plato is idealistic, Aristotle is more pragmatic.
82. Emerson is probably quoting a translation of Aristotle's *Politics*, Book III, Part XIII.
83. Pronounced sek-TEHR-ee-uhn. A member of a sect (a group within religion that has separated itself from the established church).
84. Pronounced in-EK-zer-uh-bull. Impossible to sway.

34   The habit of a realist to find things the reverse of their appearance inclined him to put every statement in a paradox. A certain habit of antagonism[85] defaced his earlier writings,—a trick of rhetoric not quite outgrown in his later, of substituting for the obvious word and thought its diametrical[86] opposite. He praised wild mountains and winter forests for their domestic air, in snow and ice he would find sultriness, and commended the wilderness for resembling Rome and Paris. "It was so dry, that you might call it wet."

35   The tendency to magnify the moment, to read all the laws of Nature in the one object or one combination under your eye, is of course comic to those who do not share the philosopher's perception of identity. To him there was no such thing as size. The pond was a small ocean; the Atlantic, a large Walden Pond. He referred every minute[87] fact to cosmical laws. Though he meant to be just, he seemed haunted by a certain chronic assumption that the science of the day pretended completeness, and he had just found out that the *savans*[88] had neglected to discriminate a particular botanical variety, had failed to describe the seeds or count the sepals. "That is to say," we replied, "the blockheads were not born in Concord; but who said they were? It was their unspeakable misfortune to be born in London, or Paris, or Rome; but, poor fellows, they did what they could, considering that they never saw Bateman's Pond, or Nine-Acre Corner, or Becky Stow's Swamp; besides, what were you sent into the world for, but to add this observation?"

36   Had his genius been only contemplative, he had been fitted to his life, but with his energy and practical ability he seemed born for great enterprise and for command; and I so much

---

85. Pronounced an-TAG-uh-nih-zum. Aggressive or belligerent contrariety.
86. Pronounced die-uh-MEH-trih-kuhl. Extremely opposed.
87. Pronounced mi-NYOOT/NOOT. Tiny.
88. Pronounced suh-VAHN. (Also spelled "savant.") An expert, but with the connotation of someone who memorizes without necessarily understanding.

regret the loss of his rare powers of action, that I cannot help counting it a fault in him that he had no ambition. Wanting this, instead of engineering for all America, he was the captain of a huckleberry-party. Pounding beans is good to the end of pounding empires one of these days; but if, at the end of years, it is still only beans!

But these foibles,[89] real or apparent, were fast vanishing in the incessant growth of a spirit so robust and wise, and which effaced[90] its defeats with new triumphs. His study of Nature was a perpetual ornament to him, and inspired his friends with curiosity to see the world through his eyes, and to hear his adventures. They possessed every kind of interest.

He had many elegancies of his own, whilst he scoffed at conventional elegance. Thus, he could not bear to hear the sound of his own steps, the grit of gravel; and therefore never willingly walked in the road, but in the grass, on mountains and in woods. His senses were acute, and he remarked that by night every dwelling-house gives out bad air, like a slaughter-house. He liked the pure fragrance of melilot[91]. He honored certain plants with special regard, and, over all, the pond-lily,—then, the gentian, and the *Mikania scandens*,[92] and "life-everlasting," and a bass-tree which he visited every year when it bloomed, in the middle of July. He thought the scent a more oracular[93] inquisition than the sight,—more oracular and trustworthy. The scent, of course, reveals what is concealed from the other senses. By it he detected earthiness. He delighted in echoes, and said they were almost the only kind of kindred voices that he heard. He loved Nature so well, was so happy in her solitude, that he

---

89. Pronounced FOY-bullz. Flaws, with the connotation of their being silly or endearing.
90. Pronounced ih-FAYS'd. Eclipsed, wore away, hid.
91. Sweet clover.
92. A white flower in the aster family.
93. Pronounced or-AK-yuh-ler. Having to do with an oracle; prophetic.

became very jealous of cities and the sad work which their refinements and artifices made with man and his dwelling. The axe was always destroying his forest. "Thank God," he said, "they cannot cut down the clouds!" "All kinds of figures are drawn on the blue ground with this fibrous white paint."

I subjoin a few sentences taken from his unpublished manuscripts,[94] not only as records of his thought and feeling, but for their power of description and literary excellence:—

"Some circumstantial evidence is very strong, as when you find a trout in the milk."

"The chub is a soft fish, and tastes like boiled brown paper salted."

"The youth gets together his materials to build a bridge to the moon, or, perchance, a palace or temple on the earth, and, at length the middle-aged man concludes to build a wood-shed with them."

"The locust z-ing."

"Devil's-needles[95] zigzagging along the Nut-Meadow brook."

"Sugar is not so sweet to the palate as sound to the healthy ear."

"I put on some hemlock-boughs, and the rich salt crackling of their leaves was like mustard to the ear, the crackling of uncountable regiments. Dead trees love the fire."

"The bluebird carries the sky on his back."

"The tanager flies through the green foliage as if it would ignite the leaves."

---

94. Both Thoreau and Emerson kept journals to record their thoughts and observations. Thoreau wrote regularly in his for more than twenty years! Many of Thoreau's letters have also been preserved.

95. This and "the Devil's darning needle" were terms for the dragonfly.

49 "If I wish for a horse-hair[96] for my compass-sight I must go to the stable; but the hair-bird, with her sharp eyes, goes to the road."

50 "Immortal water, alive even to the superficies."

51 "Fire is the most tolerable third party."

52 "Nature made ferns for pure leaves, to show what she could do in that line."

53 "No tree has so fair a bole[97] and so handsome an instep as the beech."

54 "How did these beautiful rainbow-tints get into the shell of the fresh-water clam, buried in the mud at the bottom of our dark river?"

55 "Hard are the times when the infant's shoes are second-foot."

56 "We are strictly confined to our men to whom we give liberty."

57 "Nothing is so much to be feared as fear. Atheism may comparatively be popular with God himself."

58 "Of what significance the things you can forget? A little thought is sexton to all the world."

59 "How can we expect a harvest of thought who have not had a seed-time of character?"

60 "Only he can be trusted with gifts who can present a face of bronze to expectations."

61 "I ask to be melted. You can only ask of the metals that they be tender to the fire that melts them. To nought else can they be tender."

62 There is a flower known to botanists, one of the same genus with our summer plant called "Life-Everlasting," a *Gnaphalium*[98] like that, which grows on the most inaccessible cliffs of the

---

96. Early surveyors' compasses used a horse hair as part of the sighting mechanism.
97. Sounds like "bowl." Tree trunk.
98. Another relative of the sunflower.

Tyrolese[99] mountains, where the chamois[100] dare hardly venture, and which the hunter, tempted by its beauty, and by his love (for it is immensely valued by the Swiss maidens), climbs the cliffs to gather, and is sometimes found dead at the foot, with the flower in his hand. It is called by botanists the *Gnaphalium leontopodium*, but by the Swiss *Edelweisse*,[101] which signifies *Noble Purity*. Thoreau seemed to me living in the hope to gather this plant, which belonged to him of right. The scale on which his studies proceeded was so large as to require longevity, and we were the less prepared for his sudden disappearance. The country knows not yet, or in the least part, how great a son it has lost. It seems an injury that he should leave in the midst his broken task which none else can finish, a kind of indignity to so noble a soul that he should depart out of Nature before yet he has been really shown to his peers for what he is. But he, at least, is content. His soul was made for the noblest society; he had in a short life exhausted the capabilities of this world; wherever there is knowledge, wherever there is virtue, wherever there is beauty, he will find a home

99. A region of the Alps in Austria and Italy.
100. Pronounced SHA-mees or sham-WA. An animal similar to a goat or antelope.
101. A relative of the daisy.

ABOVE: Emerson's study, illustrated by Louis K. Harlow in *Haunts of Emerson*, 1889.
LEFT: Sketch of Emerson in his later years, by Otto J. Schneider.

— **1870** *publishes* both "Courage" and "Success" in a collection of essays named *Society and Solitude*

— **1871** *begins* to suffer lapses of memory

— **1872** house catches fire and burns

— **1872–1873** *travels* to Europe with his daughter

— **1875** *publishes* final collection of essays, called *Letters and Social Aims*

— **1882** *dies* April 27

"The Old Manse," from *Old Concord*, illustrated by Lester G. Hornby, published 1915.

COURAGE

Editor's Note: This lecture was given at the Boston Music Hall in November 1859. Although Emerson may not have known it, at the same time, John Brown was on trial in Virginia.

1

So nigh is grandeur to our dust,
So near is God to man,
When Duty whispers low, *Thou must*,
The youth replies, *I can.*

2

PERIL around, all else appalling,
Cannon in front and leaden rain,
Him duty, through the clarion[1] calling
To the van,[2] called not in vain.[3]

3

I OBSERVE that there are three qualities which conspicuously attract the wonder and reverence of mankind:—

4

1. Disinterestedness, as shown in indifference to the ordinary bribes and influences of conduct,—a purpose so sincere and generous that it cannot be tempted aside by any prospects of wealth or other private advantage. Self-love is, in

---

1. Pronounced CLARE-ee-un. Trumpet.
2. Refers to a "vanguard," the front group in an army.
3. This epigraph is from Emerson's poem "Voluntaries" (1863), written to commemorate a group of volunteer soldiers who fought for the Union in the Civil War.

almost all men, such an over-weight,[4] that they are incredulous of a man's habitual preference of the general good to his own; but when they see it proved by sacrifices of ease, wealth, rank, and of life itself, there is no limit to their admiration. This has made the power of the saints of the East and West, who have led the religion of great nations. Self-sacrifice is the real miracle out of which all the reported miracles grew. This makes the renown of the heroes of Greece and Rome,—of Socrates, Aristides[5] and Phocion[6]; of Quintus Curtius,[7] Cato[8] and Regulus[9]; of Hatem Tai's[10] hospitality; of Chatham,[11] whose scornful magnanimity gave him immense popularity; of Washington, giving his service to the public without salary or reward.

2. Practical power. Men admire the man who can organize their wishes and thoughts in stone and wood and steel and brass,—the man who can build the boat, who has the impiety to make the rivers run the way he wants them; who can lead his telegraph through the ocean from shore to shore; who, sitting in his closet, can lay out the plans of a campaign, sea-war and land-war, such that the best generals and admirals, when all is done, see that they must thank him for success; the power of better combination and foresight, however exhibited, whether it only plays a game of chess, or whether, more loftily, a cunning mathematician, penetrating the cubic weights of stars, predicts

---

4. A burden.
5. Aristides (c. 530–468 BC), an Athenian statesman.
6. See Phocion footnote on page 38.
7. Quintus Curtius, a Roman historian in the first century who wrote about Alexander the Great.
8. Cato the Younger (95–46 BC), a Roman statesman at the time of Julius Caesar.
9. Probably Marcus Atilius Regulus (c. 307–250 BC), a statesman, general, and consul of the Roman Republic; he was posthumously remembered as a model of heroic endurance and civic virtue.
10. Also spelled "Hatim of Tayy." A sixth-century poet from present-day Saudi Arabia mentioned in the writings of Muhammad and the tales of Arabian Nights. He was renowned across the ancient world for his generosity.
11. See Chatham footnote on page 19.

the planet which eyes had never seen; or whether, exploring the chemical elements whereof we and the world are made, and seeing their secret, Franklin draws off the lightning in his hand; suggesting that one day a wiser geology shall make the earthquake harmless and the volcano an agricultural resource. Or here is one who, seeing the wishes of men, knows how to come at their end; whispers to this friend, argues down that adversary, moulds society to his purpose, and looks at all men as wax for his hands; takes command of them as the wind does of clouds, as the mother does of the child, or the man that knows more does of the man that knows less, and leads them in glad surprise to the very point where they would be: this man is followed with acclamation.

3. The third excellence is courage, the perfect will, which no terrors can shake, which is attracted by frowns or threats or hostile armies, nay, needs these to awake and fan its reserved energies into a pure flame, and is never quite itself until the hazard is extreme; then it is serene and fertile, and all its powers play well. There is a Hercules, an Achilles, a Rustem,[12] an Arthur[13] or a Cid[14] in the mythology of every nation; and in authentic history, a Leonidas,[15] a Scipio,[16] a Cæsar, a Richard

---

12. Also spelled "Rostam." A hero in Iranian mythology.
13. King Arthur. See *Shakspeare* footnote 16.
14. Rodrigo Diaz de Vivar (c. 1043–1099), also known as El Cid, a Spanish military leader and hero in the epic poem *Cantar de Mio Cid*.
15. Leonidas I (d. 480 BC). The Spartan king and leader of the famous last stand of 300 Spartans against a Persian army of 100,000–150,000 men at the Battle of Thermopylae.
16. See Scipio footnote on page 21.

Cœur de Lion,[17] a Cromwell,[18] a Nelson,[19] a Great Condé,[20] a Bertrand du Guesclin,[21] a Doge Dandolo,[22] a Napoleon,[23] a Masséna,[24] and Ney[25]. 'Tis said courage is common, but the immense esteem in which it is held proves it to be rare. Animal resistance, the instinct of the male animal when cornered, is no doubt common; but the pure article, courage with eyes, courage with conduct, self-possession at the cannon's mouth, cheerfulness in lonely adherence to the right, is the endowment of elevated characters. I need not show how much it is esteemed, for the people give it the first rank. They forgive everything to it. What an ado[26] we make through two thousand years about Thermopylæ[27] and Salamis[28]! What a memory of Poitiers[29] and

---

17. King Richard I of England, also known as Richard the Lion-Hearted (1157–1199), fought the Turks for Jerusalem during the time of the Crusades.
18. Oliver Cromwell (1599–1658), an English revolutionary and leader who overthrew King Charles I in the First English Civil War.
19. Horatio Nelson (1758–1805), a British admiral who famously defeated Napoleon's navy at the Battle of Trafalgar.
20. Louis de Bourbon (1621–1686), a French general who fought in the Thirty Years' War.
21. Guesclin (c. 1320–1380), a French commander from Brittany during the Hundred Years' War.
22. Enrico Dandolo (c. 1107–1205), an Italian doge (elected leader) of Venice who participated in the Fourth Crusade.
23. Napoleon Bonaparte (1769–1821), a brilliant French military leader and Emperor of France from 1804 to 1814.
24. André Masséna (1758–1817), a French commander during the French Revolution and Napoleonic Wars.
25. Michel Ney (1769–1815), a commander during the French Revolution and Napoleonic Wars.
26. Pronounced uh-DOO. Fuss.
27. From the Greek words *thermós*, meaning "hot," and *pýles*, meaning "gates." Thermopylae is a Greek coastal passage known for a battle that took place there between the Greeks and Persians in 480 BC.
28. An island near Athens. The Battle of Salamis was a naval battle fought by the Greek and Persian navies in 480 BC in which the outnumbered Greeks again halted the Persian invasion after the battle of Thermopylae.
29. A French city where the Hundred Years' War's Battle of Poitiers took place in 1356.

Crécy,[30] and Bunker Hill, and Washington's endurance! And any man who puts his life in peril in a cause which is esteemed becomes the darling of all men. The very nursery-books, the ballads which delight boys, the romances which delight men, the favorite topics of eloquence, the thunderous emphasis which orators give to every martial[31] defiance and passage of arms, and which the people greet, may testify. How short a time since this whole nation rose every morning to read or to hear the traits of courage of its sons and brothers in the field, and was never weary of the theme! We have had examples of men who, for showing effective courage on a single occasion, have become a favorite spectacle to nations, and must be brought in chariots to every mass meeting.

7

Men are so charmed with valor that they have pleased themselves with being called lions, leopards, eagles and dragons, from the animals contemporary with us in the geologic formations.[32] But the animals have great advantage of us in precocity[33]. Touch the snapping-turtle with a stick, and he seizes it with his teeth. Cut off his head, and the teeth will not let go the stick. Break the egg of the young, and the little embryo, before yet the eyes are open, bites fiercely; these vivacious creatures contriving—shall we say?—not only to bite after they are dead, but also to bite before they are born.

8

But man begins life helpless. The babe is in paroxysms[34] of fear the moment its nurse leaves it alone, and it comes so slowly to any power of self-protection that mothers say the salvation of the life and health of a young child is a perpetual

---

30. The site of 1346 battle in the Hundred Years' War.
31. Pronounced MAR-shuhl. Having to do with war.
32. Emerson may referring to the scientific theories of Charles Lyell (1797–1875), who wrote *Principles of Geology*. This book suggested uniformitarianism, in which slow, gradual changes account for the layers of Earth's surface and its fossil record.
33. Pronounced prih-KAH-sih-tee. Biologically, precocity refers to a rapid maturity and mobility from the moment of birth.
34. Pronounced PEHR-uk-sihz-um or puh-ROK-sihz-umz. Violent fits of emotion.

miracle. The terrors of the child are quite reasonable, and add to his loveliness; for his utter ignorance and weakness, and his enchanting indignation on such a small basis of capital compel every by-stander to take his part. Every moment as long as he is awake he studies the use of his eyes, ears, hands and feet, learning how to meet and avoid his dangers, and thus every hour loses one terror more. But this education stops too soon. A large majority of men being bred in families and beginning early to be occupied day by day with some routine of safe industry, never come to the rough experiences that make the Indian, the soldier or the frontiersman self-subsistent and fearless. Hence the high price of courage indicates the general timidity. "Mankind," said Franklin,[35] "are dastardly when they meet with opposition."[36] In war even generals are seldom found eager to give battle. Lord Wellington[37] said, "Uniforms were often masks;" and again, "When my journal appears, many statues must come down." The Norse Sagas[38] relate that when Bishop Magne reproved King Sigurd for his wicked divorce, the priest who attended the bishop, expecting every moment when the savage king would burst with rage and slay his superior, said that he "saw the sky no bigger than a calf-skin." And I remember when a pair of Irish girls who had been run away with in a wagon by a skittish horse, said that when he began to rear, they were so frightened that they could not see the horse.

---

35. Benjamin Franklin (1706–1790), an American author and founding father.
36. Emerson is paraphrasing a quote from the papers of John Adams published in 1851 as *The Works of John Adams* by his son Charles Adams. In the book, the quote is spoken by a wheelwright and inventor named Viny, who says Franklin once said it to him.
37. Arthur Wellesley (1769–1852), an Irish military leader who defeated Napoleon at the Battle of Waterloo in 1815.
38. Emerson is probably referring to the Saga of Sigurd the Crusader, which is part of the *Heimskringla* collection of stories about Scandinavian kings. The collection comes from oral tradition and was written down c. 1230 by Icelandic poet Snorri Sturluson (c. 1178–1241). Norse sagas have influenced a diverse range of authors, from J. R. R. Tolkien to Ezra Pound.

9

Cowardice shuts the eyes till the sky is not larger than a calf-skin; shuts the eyes so that we cannot see the horse that is running away with us; worse, shuts the eyes of the mind and chills the heart. Fear is cruel and mean. The political reigns of terror have been reigns of madness and malignity,[39]—a total perversion of opinion; society is upside down, and its best men are thought too bad to live. Then the protection which a house, a family, neighborhood and property, even the first accumulation of savings gives, go in all times to generate this taint of the respectable classes. Those political parties which gather in the well-disposed portion of the community,—how infirm and ignoble[40]! what white lips they have! always on the defensive, as if the lead were intrusted to the journals, often written in great part by women and boys, who, without strength, wish to keep up the appearance of strength. They can do the hurras, the placarding, the flags,—and the voting, if it is a fair day; but the aggressive attitude of men who will have right done, will no longer be bothered with burglars and ruffians in the streets, counterfeiters in public offices, and thieves on the bench; that part, the part of the leader and soul of the vigilance committee, must be taken by stout and sincere men who are really angry and determined. In ordinary, we have a snappish criticism which watches and contradicts the opposite party. We want the will which advances and dictates. When we get an advantage, as in Congress the other day, it is because our adversary has committed a fault, not that we have taken the initiative and given the law. Nature has made up her mind that what cannot defend itself shall not be defended. Complaining never so loud and with never so much reason is of no use. One heard much cant[41] of peace-parties long ago in Kansas and elsewhere, that their strength lay in the greatness of their wrongs, and dissuading

---

39. Pronounced muh-LIHG-nih-tee. Something is malignant if it intends harm.
40. Pronounced ihg-NOE-bull. "Un-noble," either in birth or in deed.
41. Sounds like "can't." Insincere or whining speech; gibberish; jargon.

all resistance, as if to make this strength greater. But were their wrongs greater than the negro's? And what kind of strength did they ever give him[42]? It was always invitation to the tyrant, and bred disgust in those who would protect the victim. What cannot stand must fall; and the measure of our sincerity and therefore of the respect of men, is the amount of health and wealth we will hazard in the defence of our right. An old farmer, my neighbor across the fence, when I ask him if he is not going to town-meeting, says: "No; 't is no use balloting,[43] for it will not stay; but what you do with the gun will stay so." Nature has charged every one with his own defence as with his own support, and the only title I can have to your help is when I have manfully put forth all the means I possess to keep me, and being overborne by odds, the by-standers have a natural wish to interfere and see fair play.

But with this pacific[44] education we have no readiness for bad times. I am much mistaken if every man who went to the army in the late war had not a lively curiosity to know how he should behave in action. Tender, amiable boys, who had never encountered any rougher play than a base-ball match or a fishing excursion, were suddenly drawn up to face a bayonet[45] charge or capture a battery[46]. Of course they must each go into that action with a certain despair. Each whispers to himself: "My exertions must be of small account to the result; only will the benignant[47] Heaven save me from disgracing myself and my

---

42. These questions allude to those asked by John Brown in the Concord Town Hall during the debate about whether Kansas would be admitted to the union as a slave or free state.
43. Pronounced BA-luht-eeng. Voting.
44. Peaceful or peace-making. From the Latin *pax* (genitive singular *pacis*), meaning "peace."
45. Bayonets are knives or swords on the ends of rifles.
46. A company of soldiers, a frame for mounted cannons, or a fortified position that protects soldiers.
47. Pronounced b'NIHG-nunt. Benign, kindly.

friends and my State. Die! O yes, I can well die; but I cannot afford to misbehave; and I do not know how I shall feel." So great a soldier as the old French Marshal Montluc[48] acknowledges that he has often trembled with fear, and recovered courage when he had said a prayer for the occasion. I knew a young soldier who died in the early campaign, who confided to his sister that he had made up his mind to volunteer for the war. "I have not," he said, "any proper courage, but I shall never let any one find it out." And he had accustomed himself always to go into whatever place of danger, and do whatever he was afraid to do, setting a dogged resolution to resist this natural infirmity. Coleridge has preserved an anecdote of an officer in the British Navy who told him that when he, in his first boat expedition, a midshipman[49] in his fourteenth year, accompanied Sir Alexander Ball,[50] "as we were rowing up to the vessel we were to attack, amid a discharge of musketry, I was overpowered with fear, my knees shook and I was ready to faint away. Lieutenant Ball seeing me, placed himself close beside me, took hold of my hand and whispered, 'Courage, my dear boy! you will recover in a minute or so; I was just the same when I first went out in this way.' It was as if an angel spoke to me. From that moment I was as fearless and as forward as the oldest of the boat's crew. But I dare not think what would have become of me, if, at that moment, he had scoffed and exposed me."[51]

11 Knowledge is the antidote to fear,—Knowledge, Use and Reason, with its higher aids. The child is as much in danger from a staircase, or the fire-grate, or a bath-tub, or a cat, as the soldier from a cannon or an ambush. Each surmounts the fear as fast

---

48. Blaise de Montluc (1502–1577), a French knight who fought for King Francis I and Henry III.
49. Pronounced mid-SHIP-mun. A navy trainee/student.
50. Ball (1757–1809), a British naval officer. The poet Samuel Coleridge was his secretary during Ball's time as governor of Malta, an island south of Italy.
51. This anecdote comes from an essay in Coleridge's *The Friend* (first a periodical, then a collection of essays).

as he precisely understands the peril and learns the means of resistance. Each is liable[52] to panic, which is, exactly, the terror of ignorance surrendered to the imagination. Knowledge is the encourager, knowledge that takes fear out of the heart, knowledge and use, which is knowledge in practice. They can conquer who believe they can. It is he who has done the deed once who does not shrink from attempting it again. It is the groom who knows the jumping horse well who can safely ride him. It is the veteran soldier, who, seeing the flash of the cannon, can step aside from the path of the ball. Use makes a better soldier than the most urgent considerations of duty,—familiarity with danger enabling him to estimate the danger. He sees how much is the risk, and is not afflicted with imagination; knows practically Marshal Saxe's[53] rule, that every soldier killed costs the enemy his weight in lead.

12

The sailor loses fear as fast as he acquires command of sails and spars and steam; the frontiersman, when he has a perfect rifle and has acquired a sure aim. To the sailor's experience every new circumstance suggests what he must do. The terrific chances which make the hours and the minutes long to the passenger, he whiles away by incessant application of expedients and repairs. To him a leak, a hurricane, or a waterspout is so much work,— no more. The hunter is not alarmed by bears, catamounts[54] or wolves, nor the grazier[55] by his bull, nor the dog-breeder by his bloodhound, nor an Arab by the simoo[m],[56] nor a farmer by a fire in the woods. The forest on fire looks discouraging enough to a citizen: the farmer is skilful to fight it. The neighbors run together; with pine boughs they can mop out the flame, and by

---

52. Pronounced LIE-uh-bull. Prone, likely.
53. Maurice, Count of Saxony (1696–1750), a German military leader who served under Peter the Great and Emperor Charles VI.
54. Pronounced KAT-uh-mounts. Mountain lions.
55. Pronounced GRAY-zhyer. Someone who grazes cattle.
56. Pronounced sih-MOOM. A dust storm of the African and Asian deserts.

raking with the hoe a long but little trench, confine to a patch the fire which would easily spread over a hundred acres.

13 In short, courage consists in equality to the problem before us. The school-boy is daunted before his tutor by a question of arithmetic, because he does not yet command the simple steps of the solution which the boy beside him has mastered. These once seen, he is as cool as Archimedes,[57] and cheerily proceeds a step farther. Courage is equality to the problem, in affairs, in science, in trade, in council, or in action; consists in the conviction that the agents with whom you contend are not superior in strength of resources or spirit to you. The general must stimulate the mind of his soldiers to the perception that they are men, and the enemy is no more. Knowledge, yes; for the danger of dangers is illusion. The eye is easily daunted; and the drums, flags, shining helmets, beard and moustache of the soldier have conquered you long before his sword or bayonet reaches you.

14 But we do not exhaust the subject in the slight analysis; we must not forget the variety of temperaments, each of which qualifies this power of resistance. It is observed that men with little imagination are less fearful; they wait till they feel pain, whilst others of more sensibility anticipate it, and suffer in the fear of the pang more acutely than in the pang. 'T is certain that the threat is sometimes more formidable than the stroke, and 't is possible that the beholders suffer more keenly than the victims. Bodily pain is superficial, seated usually in the skin and the extremities, for the sake of giving us warning to put us on our guard; not in the vitals, where the rupture that produces death is perhaps not felt, and the victim never knew what hurt him. Pain is superficial, and therefore fear is. The torments of martyrdoms are probably most keenly felt by the by-standers. The torments are illusory. The first suffering is the last suffering,

---

57. Archimedes (c. 287–c. 212 BC), a Greek mathematician and physicist who famously exclaimed "Eureka!" ("I found it!") when he discovered how to measure the volume of an irregular solid.

the later hurts being lost on insensibility. Our affections and wishes for the external welfare of the hero tumultuously[58] rush to expression in tears and outcries: but we, like him, subside into indifferency and defiance when we perceive how short is the longest arm of malice, how serene is the sufferer.

15 It is plain that there is no separate essence called courage, no cup or cell in the brain, no vessel in the heart containing drops or atoms that make or give this virtue; but it is the right or healthy state of every man, when he is free to do that which is constitutional to him to do. It is directness,—the instant performing of that which he ought. The thoughtful man says, You differ from me in opinion and methods, but do you not see that I cannot think or act otherwise than I do? that my way of living is organic[59]? And to be really strong we must adhere to our own means. On organic action all strength depends. Hear what women say of doing a task by sheer force of will: it costs them a fit of sickness. Plutarch relates that the Pythoness[60] who tried to prophesy without command in the Temple at Delphi, though she performed the usual rites, and inhaled the air of the cavern standing on the tripod, fell into convulsions and died. Undoubtedly there is a temperamental courage, a warlike blood, which loves a fight, does not feel itself except in a quarrel, as one sees in wasps, or ants, or cocks, or cats. The like vein appears in certain races of men and in individuals of every race. In every school there are certain fighting boys; in every society, the contradicting men; in every town, bravoes[61] and bullies, better or worse dressed, fancy-men, patrons of the cock-pit[62] and the ring. Courage is temperamental, scientific, ideal. Swedenborg[63]

---

58. Pronounced tuh-MUHL-choo-uss-lee. In a rough, unsettled fashion.
59. Natural.
60. The Oracle of Delphi, and a priestess of the god Apollo in Greek mythology.
61. Pronounced BRAH-voez. Villains, bandits.
62. Cockfighting was brutal sport where two male birds, often roosters, were placed in a small ring called a "cock-pit" and forced to fight.
63. See footnote on page 34.

COURAGE

has left this record of his king: "Charles XII. of Sweden did not know what that was which others called fear, nor what that spurious[64] valor and daring that is excited by inebriating[65] draughts, for he never tasted any liquid but pure water. Of him we may say that he led a life more remote from death, and in fact lived more, than any other man." It was told of the Prince of Condé that "there not being a more furious man in the world, danger in fight never disturbs him more than just to make him civil, and to command in words of great obligation to his officers and men, and without any the least disturbance to his judgment or spirit."[66] Each has his own courage, as his own talent; but the courage of the tiger is one, and of the horse another. The dog that scorns to fight, will fight for his master. The llama that will carry a load if you caress him, will refuse food and die if he is scourged. The fury of onset is one, and of calm endurance another. There is a courage of the cabinet as well as a courage of the field; a courage of manners in private assemblies, and another in public assemblies; a courage which enables one man to speak masterly to a hostile company, whilst another man who can easily face a cannon's mouth dares not open his own.

16 There is a courage of a merchant in dealing with his trade, by which dangerous turns of affairs are met and prevailed over. Merchants recognize as much gallantry, well judged too, in the conduct of a wise and upright man of business in difficult times, as soldiers in a soldier.

17 There is a courage in the treatment of every art by a master in architecture, in sculpture, in painting or in poetry, each cheering the mind of the spectator or receiver as by true strokes of genius, which yet nowise[67] implies the presence of physical valor in the artist. This is the courage of genius, in every kind. A

---

64. Pronounced SPER-ee-uss. Deceitful
65. Pronounced ih-NEE-bree-ay-teeng. Intoxicating.
66. From the diary of Samuel Pepys (1663–1703), entry dated Saturday, June 4, 1664.
67. In no way.

certain quantity of power belongs to a certain quantity of faculty. The beautiful voice at church goes sounding on, and covers up in its volume, as in a cloak, all the defects of the choir. The singers, I observe, all yield to it, and so the fair singer indulges her instinct, and dares, and dares, because she knows she can.

It gives the cutting edge to every profession. The judge puts his mind to the tangle of contradictions in the case, squarely accosts the question, and by not being afraid of it, by dealing with it as business which must be disposed of, he sees presently that common arithmetic and common methods apply to this affair. Perseverance strips it of all peculiarity, and ranges it on the same ground as other business. Morphy[68] played a daring game in chess: the daring was only an illusion of the spectator, for the player sees his move to be well fortified and safe. You may see the same dealing in criticism; a new book astonishes for a few days, takes itself out of common jurisdiction, and nobody knows what to say of it: but the scholar is not deceived. The old principles which books exist to express are more beautiful than any book; and out of love of the reality he is an expert judge how far the book has approached it and where it has come short. In all applications it is the same power,—the habit of reference to one's own mind, as the home of all truth and counsel, and which can easily dispose of any book because it can very well do without all books. When a confident man comes into a company magnifying this or that author he has freshly read, the company grow silent and ashamed of their ignorance. But I remember the old professor,[69] whose searching mind engraved every word he spoke on the memory of the class, when we asked if he had read this or that shining novelty, "No, I have never read that book;" instantly the book lost credit, and was not to be heard of again.

---

68. Paul Charles Morphy (1837–1884), a famous American prodigy and chess champion.
69. Probably Professor Andrews Norton (1786–1853) of Harvard.

Every creature has a courage of his constitution fit for his duties:—Archimedes, the courage of a geometer to stick to his diagram, heedless of the siege and sack of the city; and the Roman soldier his faculty to strike at Archimedes. Each is strong, relying on his own, and each is betrayed when he seeks in himself the courage of others.

Captain John Brown, the hero of Kansas, said to me in conversation, that "for a settler in a new country, one good, believing, strong-minded man is worth a hundred, nay, a thousand men without character; and that the right men will give a permanent direction to the fortunes of a state. As for the bullying drunkards of which armies are usually made up, he thought cholera, small-pox and consumption as valuable recruits." He held the belief that courage and chastity are silent concerning themselves. He said, "As soon as I hear one of my men say, 'Ah, let me only get my eye on such a man, I 'll bring him down,' I don't expect much aid in the fight from that talker. 'T is the quiet, peaceable men, the men of principle, that make the best soldiers."

"'T is still observed those men most valiant are
Who are most modest ere they came to war."[70]

True courage is not ostentatious; men who wish to inspire terror seem thereby to confess themselves cowards. Why do they rely on it, but because they know how potent it is with themselves?

The true temper has genial influences. It makes a bond of union between enemies. Governor Wise of Virginia,[71] in the record of his first interviews with his prisoner, appeared to great advantage. If Governor Wise is a superior man, or inasmuch as he is a superior man, he distinguishes John Brown. As they confer, they understand each other swiftly; each respects the

---

70. An aside in Robert Herrick's (1591–1674) collection of poems *Hesperides*.
71. Henry Wise (1806–1876), the thirty-third governor of Virginia, who signed John Brown's death warrant.

other. If opportunity allowed, they would prefer each other's society and desert their former companions. Enemies would become affectionate. Hector and Achilles, Richard and Saladin,[72] Wellington[73] and Soult,[74] General Daumas[75] and Abdel-Kader,[76] become aware that they are nearer and more alike than any other two, and, if their nation and circumstance did not keep them apart, would run into each other's arms.

See too what good contagion belongs to it. Everywhere it finds its own with magnetic affinity. Courage of the soldier awakes the courage of woman. Florence Nightingale[77] brings lint and the blessing of her shadow.[78] Heroic women offer themselves as nurses of the brave veteran. The troop of Virginian infantry that had marched to guard the prison of John Brown ask leave to pay their respects to the prisoner. Poetry and eloquence catch the hint, and soar to a pitch unknown before. Everything feels the new breath except the old doting nigh-dead politicians, whose heart the trumpet of resurrection could not wake.

The charm of the best courages is that they are inventions, inspirations, flashes of genius. The hero could not have done the feat at another hour, in a lower mood. The best act of the marvellous genius of Greece was its first act; not in the statue or the

---

72. Saladin (1137–1193), sultan of Egypt and Syria who led the Muslim army during the Crusades. Richard the Lionhearted defeated him in the Battle of Arsuf of 1191.
73. See footnote on page 104.
74. Marshal General Jean-de-Dieu Soult (1769–1851), a French general under Napoleon.
75. Eugene Daumas (1803–1871), a French general who served under Charles X and fought in the French colonial wars in Algeria.
76. Emir Abdelkader (1808–1883), an Algerian religious and military leader who fought against French colonialism.
77. Nightingale (1820–1910), an English woman who founded modern nursing.
78. An allusion to Henry Wadsworth Longfellow's (1807–1882) poem "Santa Filomena": "And slow, as in a dream of bliss, / The speechless sufferer turns to kiss / Her shadow, as it falls / Upon the darkening walls."

Parthenon,[79] but in the instinct which, at Thermopylæ, held Asia at bay, kept Asia out of Europe,[80]—Asia with its antiquities and organic slavery,—from corrupting the hope and new morning of the West. The statue, the architecture, were the later and inferior creation of the same genius. In view of this moment of history, we recognize a certain prophetic instinct, better than wisdom. Napoleon said well, "My hand is immediately connected with my head;" but the *sacred* courage is connected with the heart. The head is a half, a fraction, until it is enlarged and inspired by the moral sentiment. For it is not the means on which we draw, as health or wealth, practical skill or dexterous[81] talent, or multitudes of followers, that count, but the aims only. The aim reacts back on the means. A great aim aggrandizes the means. The meal and water that are the commissariat[82] of the *forlorn hope* that stake their lives to defend the pass are sacred as the Holy Grail,[83] or as if one had eyes to see in chemistry the fuel that is rushing to feed the sun.

26 There is a persuasion in the soul of man that he is here for cause, that he was put down in this place by the Creator to do the work for which he inspires him, that thus he is an overmatch for all antagonists that could combine against him. The pious[84] Mrs. Hutchinson[85] says of some passages in the defence of

---

79. The Temple of Athena, located in Athens. Its rows of columns are iconic. It has been called "the most perfect Doric temple ever built."
80. Emerson is saying that the genius of ancient Greece comes not from its art or architecture, but from its military defeat of the Persians at Thermopylae, which made space for a distinctly Greek identity.
81. Pronounced DEKS-truss. Agile, physically skilled.
82. Pronounced kah-muh-SEHR-ee-uht. Food provided for an army.
83. A mythical goblet thought to have miraculous powers sought by King Arthur. Today a "Holy Grail" is something desired above all else, the end-all-be-all of a given field.
84. Pronounced PIE-uss. Conscientiously or demonstrably religious.
85. Lucy Hutchinson (1620–1681), an English poet and biographer who wrote *Memoirs of the Life of Colonel Hutchinson, Governor of Nottingham* in 1644.

Nottingham against the Cavaliers,[86] "It was a great instruction that the best and highest courages are beams of the Almighty." And whenever the religious sentiment is adequately affirmed, it must be with dazzling courage. As long as it is cowardly insinuated, as with the wish to succor[87] some partial and temporary interest, or to make it affirm some pragmatical[88] tenet[89] which our parish church receives to-day, it is not imparted, and cannot inspire or create. For it is always new, leads and surprises, and practice never comes up with it. There are ever appearing in the world men who, almost as soon as they are born, take a bee-line to the rack of the inquisitor,[90] the axe of the tyrant, like Giordano Bruno,[91] Vanini,[92] Huss,[93] Paul, Jesus and Socrates. Look at Fox's Lives of the Martyrs, Sewel's History of the Quakers,[94] Southey's Book of the Church,[95] at the folios[96] of the Brothers Bollandi,[97] who collected the lives of twenty-five thousand martyrs,

---

86. During the English Civil War (1642–1651), the Cavaliers supported the monarchy of Charles I.
87. Sounds like "sucker." Help, provide support to.
88. Pronounced prag-MA-tih-kull. Practical.
89. Pronounced TEHN-it. Belief.
90. The rack was a medieval torture tool that would stretch the limbs of its victim. An inquisitor is an interrogator, with the connotation of someone harsh and impassive.
91. Bruno (1548–1600), an Italian philosopher and mathematician who was tried for heresy.
92. Lucilio Vanini (1585–1619), an Italian philosopher and physician who was executed.
93. Probably Jan Hus (c. 1369–1415), an Czech theologian and church reformer who was also executed.
94. William Sewel (1653–1720) wrote *The History of the Rise, Increase, and Progress of the Christian People called Quakers*.
95. Robert Southey (1774–1843) wrote *The Book of the Church*, a work intended to inspire gratefulness for the church by detailing its history, accomplishments, and sacrifices.
96. Pronounced FOE-lee-oze. Folded pages of a manuscript bound into a book; often a synonym for "book."
97. Bollandists are followers of Flemish Priest Jean Bolland (1596–1665) and are dedicated to the study of saints. It took over three hundred years to complete the sixty-eight volume encyclopedia of saints' lives called *Acta Sanctorum*.

COURAGE

confessors, ascetics and self-tormentors. There is much of fable, but a broad basis of fact. The tender skin does not shrink from bayonets, the timid woman is not scared by fagots[98]; the rack is not frightful, nor the rope ignominious[99]. The poor Puritan, Antony Parsons,[100] at the stake, tied straw on his head when the fire approached him, and said, "This is God's hat." Sacred courage indicates that a man loves an idea better than all things in the world; that he is aiming neither at pelf[101] nor comfort, but will venture all to put in act the invisible thought in his mind. He is everywhere a liberator, but of a freedom that is ideal; not seeking to have land or money or conveniences, but to have no other limitation than that which his own constitution imposes. He is free to speak truth; he is not free to lie. He wishes to break every yoke all over the world which hinders his brother from acting after his thought.

27 There are degrees of courage, and each step upward makes us acquainted with a higher virtue. Let us say then frankly that the education of the will is the object of our existence. Poverty, the prison, the rack, the fire, the hatred and execrations[102] of our fellow men, appear trials beyond the endurance of common humanity; but to the hero whose intellect is aggrandized by the soul, and so measures these penalties against the good which his thought surveys, these terrors vanish as darkness at sunrise.

28 We have little right in piping times of peace to pronounce on these rare heights of character[103]; but there is no assurance

---

98. Pronounced FA-guht. A bundle of sticks.
99. Pronounced ihg-nuh-MIHN-ee-uss. Shameful.
100. Anthony Parsons is referenced in *Foxe's Book of Martyrs*.
101. Pronounced PEHLF. Wealth.
102. Pronounced ehks-uh-KRAY-shunz. To execrate something is to denounce it, curse it, or claim it to be evil.
103. "Pronounce" here meaning "to preach" or "to speak." Emerson is saying it might seem odd to preach on courage in peaceful times. Also a reference to Shakespeare's *Richard III*, where in the opening monologue, Richard speaks of "this weak piping time of peace."

of security. In the most private life, difficult duty is never far off. Therefore we must think with courage. Scholars and thinkers are prone to an effeminate habit, and shrink if a coarser shout comes up from the street, or a brutal act is recorded in the journals. The Medical College[104] piles up in its museum its grim monsters of morbid anatomy, and there are melancholy skeptics with a taste for carrion[105] who batten[106] on the hideous facts in history,—persecutions, inquisitions,[107] St. Bartholomew massacres,[108] devilish lives, Nero,[109] Cæsar Borgia,[110] Marat,[111] Lopez[112]; men in whom every ray of humanity was extinguished, parricides,[113] matricides[114] and whatever moral monsters. These are not cheerful facts, but they do not disturb a healthy mind; they require of us a patience as robust as the energy that attacks us, and an unresting exploration of final causes[115]. Wolf, snake and crocodile are not inharmonious in Nature, but are made useful as checks, scavengers and pioneers; and we must have a scope as large as Nature's to deal with beast-like men, detect what

---

104. Emerson may be referring to the Harvard Medical School, his alma mater. The Warren Anatopical Museum was founded there in 1847.
105. Pronounced KEHR-ee-uhn. Rot, or, specifically, rotting flesh (e.g., dead animals eaten by buzzards).
106. Pronounced BAT'n. Gorge (themselves).
107. The Inquisitions (from the early 1200s to the early 1800s) were operations designed to combat "heresy" in Catholic countries. Inquisitors would interrogate people and mete out punishments for perceived heretics, sometimes punishments as harsh as burning at the stake.
108. In Paris, 1572, the Catholic Catherine de'Medici, mother of King Charles IX, allowed or instigated a masssacre of French protestants known as the Huguenots.
109. Nero (37–68 AD), a Roman emperor who persecuted Christians.
110. Borgia (1415–1507), an Italian military leader admired by Niccolò Machiavelli, father of modern political science.
111. Jean-Paul Marat (1743–1793), a French scientist and revolutionary assassinated during the French Revolution.
112. Possibly Antonio Lopez de Santa Anna (1794–1876), a Mexican general and dictator-president of Texas before his defeat by Sam Houston.
113. Pronounced PEHR-ih-sidez. The killing of one's parents.
114. Pronounced MA-truh-sidez. The killing of one's mother.
115. See footnote about Aristotle's Four Causes on page 90.

scullion[116] function is assigned them, and foresee in the secular melioration[117] of the planet how these will become unnecessary and will die out.

29 He has not learned the lesson of life who does not every day surmount a fear. I do not wish to put myself or any man into a theatrical position, or urge him to ape[118] the courage of his comrade. Have the courage not to adopt another's courage. There is scope and cause and resistance enough for us in our proper work and circumstance. And there is no creed of an honest man, be he Christian, Turk or Gentoo,[119] which does not equally preach it. If you have no faith in beneficent power above you, but see only an adamantine[120] fate coiling its folds about Nature and man, then reflect that the best use of fate is to teach us courage, if only because baseness cannot change the appointed event. If you accept your thoughts as inspirations from the Supreme Intelligence, obey them when they prescribe difficult duties, because they come only so long as they are used; or, if your skepticism reaches to the last verge, and you have no confidence in any foreign mind, then be brave, because there is one good opinion which must always be of consequence to you, namely, your own.

30 I am permitted to enrich my chapter by adding an anecdote of pure courage from real life, as narrated in a ballad by a lady[121] to whom all the particulars of the fact are exactly known.

---

116. Pronounced SKUHL-yuhn. A scullion is a kitchen servant. Here, Emerson uses it as an adjective to mean lowly or menial.
117. Pronouonced MEE-lee-uh-ray-shunz. Measures taken to make something better, easier, less painful.
118. Mimic crudely.
119. Pronounced JEHN-too. Hindu.
120. Pronounced ad-uh-MAN-teen. Extremely hard, solid.
121. From Elizabeth Hoar's (see footnote on page 77) "Ballad of George Nidever."

31 GEORGE NIDIVER[122]

32

Men have done brave deeds,
  And bards have sung them well:
I of good George Nidiver
  Now the tale will tell.

33

In Californian mountains
  A hunter bold was he:
Keen his eye and sure his aim
  As any you should see.

34

A little Indian boy
  Followed him everywhere,
Eager to share the hunter's joy,
  The hunter's meal to share.

35

And when the bird or deer
  Fell by the hunter's skill,
The boy was always near
  To help with right good will.

36

One day as through the cleft
  Between two mountains steep,
Shut in both right and left,
  Their questing way they keep,

37

They see two grizzly bears
  With hunger fierce and fell
Rush at them unawares
  Right down the narrow dell.

38

The boy turned round with screams,
  And ran with terror wild;

---

122. Nidiver/Nidever (1802–1883), a notorious explorer, trapper, and sailor in California after Mexican-American War.

COURAGE

One of the pair of savage beasts
  Pursued the shrieking child.

The hunter raised his gun,—
  He knew one charge was all,—
And through the boy's pursuing foe
  He sent his only ball.

The other on George Nidiver
  Came on with dreadful pace:
The hunter stood unarmed,
  And met him face to face.

I say unarmed he stood.
  Against those frightful paws
The rifle butt, or club of wood,
  Could stand no more than straws.

George Nidiver stood still
  And looked him in the face;
The wild beast stopped amazed,
  Then came with slackening pace.

Still firm the hunter stood,
  Although his heart beat high;
Again the creature stopped,
  And gazed with wondering eye.

The hunter met his gaze,
  Nor yet an inch gave way;
The bear turned slowly round,
  And slowly moved away.

What thoughts were in his mind
  It would be hard to spell:
What thoughts were in George Nidiver
  I rather guess than tell.

46

    But sure that rifle's aim,
      Swift choice of generous part,
    Showed in its passing gleam
      The depths of a brave heart.

SUCCESS

    ONE thing is forever good;   **1**
That one thing is Success,—
Dear to the Eumenides,[1]
And to all the heavenly brood[2].
Who bides at home, nor looks abroad,
Carries the eagles and masters the sword.[3]

    BUT if thou do thy best,   **2**
Without remission, without rest,
And invite the sunbeam,
And abhor to feign or seem
Even to those who thee should love
And thy behavior approve;
If thou go in thine own likeness,
Be it health or be it sickness;
If thou go as thy father's son,
If thou wear no mask or lie,
    Dealing purely and nakedly;—[4]

---

1. Another name for the Greek Furies, goddesses of vengeance who punish people who break their oaths.
2. Rhymes with "rude." A group of offspring.
3. From the poem "Destiny" by Emerson.
4. From the poem "Life" by Emerson, found in *Fragments of Nature and Life*.

3 OUR American people cannot be taxed with slowness in performance or in praising their performance. The earth is shaken by our engineries[5]. We are feeling our youth and nerve and bone. We have the power of territory and of seacoast, and know the use of these. We count our census, we read our growing valuations, we survey our map, which becomes old in a year or two. Our eyes run approvingly along the lengthened lines of railroad and telegraph. We have gone nearest to the Pole. We have discovered the Antarctic continent. We interfere in Central and South America, at Canton[6] and in Japan; we are adding to an already enormous territory. Our political constitution is the hope of the world, and we value ourselves on all these feats.

4 'T is the way of the world; 't is the law of youth, and of unfolding strength. Men are made each with some triumphant superiority, which, through some adaptation of fingers or ear or eye or ciphering[7] or pugilistic[8] or musical or literary craft, enriches the community with a new art; and not only we, but all men of European stock, value these certificates. Giotto[9] could draw a perfect circle: Erwin of Steinbach[10] could build a minster[11]; Olaf, king of Norway,[12] could run round his galley on the blades of the oars of the rowers when the ship was in

---

5. Pronounced IHN-jihn-reez. Machinery of war.
6. A city in southern China, also called Guangzhou.
7. Pronounced SIE-fer-eeng. Doing math, working with figures and equations.
8. Pronounced pyoo-juh-LIST-ihk. Having to do with boxing or martial arts.
9. Giotto di Bondone (1267–1337), an Italian painter.
10. Erwin von Steinbach (1244–1318), a German architect.
11. Pronounced MIHN-ster. A cathedral. Here, the Strasbourg Cathedral, designed largely by Erwin von Steinbach. From 1647–1874, it was the tallest building in the world.
12. Olaf Trygvesson (c. 960–1000). This tale is told in Longfellow's "Tales of a Wayside Inn."

motion; Ojeda[13] could run out swiftly on a plank projected from the top of a tower, turn round swiftly and come back; Evelyn[14] writes from Rome: "Bernini, the Florentine sculptor, architect, painter and poet, a little before my coming to Rome, gave a public opera, wherein he painted the scenes, cut the statues, invented the engines, composed the music, writ the comedy and built the theatre."

"There is nothing in war," said Napoleon, "which I cannot do by my own hands. If there is nobody to make gunpowder, I can manufacture it. The gun-carriages I know how to construct. If it is necessary to make cannons at the forge, I can make them. The details of working them in battle, if it is necessary to teach, I shall teach them. In administration, it is I alone who have arranged the finances, as you know."

It is recorded of Linnæus,[15] among many proofs of his beneficent skill, that when the timber in the shipyards of Sweden was ruined by rot, Linnæus was desired by the government to find a remedy. He studied the insects that infested the timber, and found that they laid their eggs in the logs within certain days in April, and he directed that during ten days at that season the logs should be immersed under water in the docks; which being done, the timber was found to be uninjured.

Columbus at Veragua[16] found plenty of gold; but leaving the coast, the ship full of one hundred and fifty skilful seamen,—some of them old pilots, and with too much experience of their craft and treachery to him,—the wise admiral kept his private

---

13. Alonso de Ojeda (1468–1515), a Spanish explorer who sailed with Christopher Columbus on his second trip to the New World and with Amerigo Vespucci, for whom the Americas are named.

14. John Evelyn (1620–1706), an English writer whose famous personal diaries offer a glimpse into everyday life of the time.

15. Carl Linnaeus (1707–1778), a Swedish botanist who created the current taxonomy system (kingdom, phylum, class, order, family, genus, species)—the Linnean system.

16. Central America.

record of his homeward path. And when he reached Spain he told the King and Queen[17] that "they may ask all the pilots who came with him where is Veragua. Let them answer and say if they know where Veragua lies. I assert that they can give no other account than that they went to lands where there was abundance of gold, but they do not know the way to return thither, but would be obliged to go on a voyage of discovery as much as if they had never been there before. There is a mode of reckoning," he proudly adds, "derived from astronomy, which is sure and safe to any one who understands it."

8

Hippocrates[18] in Greece knew how to stay the devouring plague which ravaged Athens in his time, and his skill died with him. Dr. Benjamin Rush,[19] in Philadelphia, carried that city heroically through the yellow fever[20] of the year 1793. Leverrier[21] carried the Copernican system[22] in his head, and knew where to look for the new planet. We have seen an American woman write a novel of which a million copies were sold,[23] in all languages, and which had one merit, of speaking to the universal heart, and was read with equal interest to three audiences, namely, in the parlor, in the kitchen and in the nursery of every house. We have seen women who could institute hospitals and schools in armies. We have seen a woman who by pure song could melt

---

17. Ferdinand II and Isabella I of current-day Spain.
18. Hippocrates (c. 460–377 BC), the Greek "father of medicine," from whom we get the Hippocratic Oath.
19. Benjamin Rush (1736–1813), an American doctor, politician, and social reformer who founded Dickinson College and also signed the Declaration of Independence.
20. A disease common in southern Africa and South America. Its symptoms include fever, headache, and sometimes jaundice, which gives the skin and eyes a yellow tint.
21. Urbain Le Verrier (1811–1877), a French astronomer and mathematician.
22. See the Copernicus footnote on page 18.
23. Harriet Beecher Stowe (1811–1896), who wrote the abolitionist novel *Uncle Tom's Cabin*.

the souls of whole populations.[24] And there is no limit to these varieties of talent.

These are arts to be thankful for,—each one as it is a new direction of human power. We cannot choose but respect them. Our civilization is made up of a million contributions of this kind. For success, to be sure we esteem it a test in other people, since we do first in ourselves. We respect ourselves more if we have succeeded. Neither do we grudge to each of these benefactors the praise or the profit which accrues from his industry.

Here are already quite different degrees of moral merit in these examples. I don't know but we and our race elsewhere set a higher value on wealth, victory and coarse superiority of all kinds, than other men,—have less tranquillity of mind, are less easily contented. The Saxon is taught from his infancy to wish to be first. The Norseman was a restless rider, fighter, free-booter. The ancient Norse ballads describe him as afflicted with this inextinguishable thirst of victory. The mother says to her son:—

> "Success shall be in thy courser tall,
> Success in thyself, which is best of all,
> Success in thy hand, success in thy foot,
> In struggle with man, in battle with brute:—
> The holy God and Saint Drothin[25] dear
> Shall never shut eyes on thy career;
> Look out, look out, Svend Vonved!"[26]

These feats that we extol do not signify so much as we say. These boasted arts are of very recent origin. They are local conveniences, but do not really add to our stature. The greatest men of the world have managed not to want them. Newton was a great man, without telegraph, or gas, or steam-coach, or

---

24. Jenny Lind (1820–1887), known as "the Swedish Nightingale," an incredibly talented opera singer.
25. Also called Dothin, Dotton, or Drotten. Probably refers to Jesus.
26. From the poem "Svend Vonved" translated by George Borrow (1803–1881).

rubber shoes, or lucifer-matches,[27] or ether for his pain; so was Shakspeare and Alfred[28] and Scipio and Socrates. These are local conveniences, but how easy to go now to parts of the world where not only all these arts are wanting, but where they are despised. The Arabian sheiks,[29] the most dignified people in the planet, do not want them; yet have as much self-respect as the English, and are easily able to impress the Frenchman or the American who visits them with the respect due to a brave and sufficient man.

13 These feats have to be sure great difference of merit, and some of them involve power of a high kind. But the public values the invention more than the inventor does. The inventor knows there is much more and better where this came from. The public sees in it a lucrative secret. Men see the reward which the inventor enjoys, and they think, 'How shall we win that?' Cause and effect are a little tedious; how to leap to the result by short or by false means? We are not scrupulous. What we ask is victory, without regard to the cause; after the Rob Roy rule,[30] after the Napoleon rule, to be the strongest to-day,—the way of the Talleyrands,[31] prudent people, whose watches go faster than their neighbors', and who detect the first moment of decline and throw themselves on the instant on the winning side. I have heard that Nelson used to say, "Never mind the justice or the impudence, only let me succeed." Lord Brougham's[32] single duty of counsel is, "to get the prisoner clear." Fuller says 't is a maxim

---

27. An early type of match patented by Samuel Jones (though invented by Sir Isaac Holden).
28. Possibly Alfred the Great (c. 847–899), an English king who converted Viking King Guthrum to Christianity.
29. Pronounced SHEEKs. Arabian tribe leaders or chiefs.
30. A reference to Rob Roy MacGregor (1671–1734), a Scottish outlaw.
31. An allusion to the crafty French politician Charles Maurice de Talleyrand-Périgord (1754–1838). His name is now a term for very crafty, cynical diplomacy.
32. Henry Brougham (1778–1868), the British Baron of Brougham and Vaux and eventually Lord Chancellor.

of lawyers that "a crown once worn cleareth all defects of the wearer thereof." Rien ne réussit mieux que le succès.[33] And we Americans are tainted with this insanity, as our bankruptcies and our reckless politics may show. We are great by exclusion, grasping and egotism. Our success takes from all what it gives to one. 'T is a haggard, malignant, careworn running for luck.

14 Egotism is a kind of buckram[34] that gives momentary strength and concentration to men, and seems to be much used in Nature for fabrics in which local and spasmodic[35] energy is required. I could point to men in this country, of indispensable importance to the carrying on of American life, of this humor, whom we could ill spare; any one of them would be a national loss. But it spoils conversation. They will not try conclusions with you. They are ever thrusting this pampered self between you and them. It is plain they have a long education to undergo to reach simplicity and plain-dealing, which are what a wise man mainly cares for in his companion. Nature knows how to convert evil to good; Nature utilizes misers, fanatics, show-men, egotists, to accomplish her ends; but we must not think better of the foible for that. The passion for sudden success is rude and puerile,[36] just as war, cannons and executions are used to clear the ground of bad, lumpish, irreclaimable savages, but always to the damage of the conquerors.

15 I hate this shallow Americanism which hopes to get rich by credit, to get knowledge by raps on midnight tables, to learn the economy of the mind by phrenology,[37] or skill without study, or mastery without apprenticeship, or the sale of goods through pretending that they sell, or power through making believe you

---

33. French: "Nothing succeeds better than success."
34. Pronounced BUHK-rum. A stiff, heavy fabric, or here, rigidity.
35. Pronounced spaz-MAHD-ik. Having to do with spasms; sporadic.
36. Pronounced PYER'l. Childish. From the Latin *puer*, meaning "boy."
37. Pronounced fren-AH-luh-jee. The study of the shape of peoples' heads, believing that skull shape affects personality and psychology.

are powerful, or through a packed jury or caucus, bribery and "repeating" votes, or wealth by fraud. They think they have got it, but they have got something else,—a crime which calls for another crime, and another devil behind that; these are steps to suicide, infamy and the harming of mankind. We countenance each other in this life of show, puffing, advertisement and manufacture of public opinion; and excellence is lost sight of in the hunger for sudden performance and praise.

16 There was a wise man, an Italian artist, Michel Angelo, who writes thus of himself: "Meanwhile the Cardinal Ippolito,[38] in whom all my best hopes were placed, being dead, I began to understand that the promises of this world are for the most part vain phantoms, and that to confide in one's self, and become something of worth and value, is the best and safest course." Now, though I am by no means sure that the reader will assent to all my propositions, yet I think we shall agree in my first rule for success,—that we shall drop the brag and the advertisement, and take Michel Angelo's course, "to confide in one's self, and be something of worth and value."

17 Each man has an aptitude born with him. Do your work. I have to say this often, but Nature says it oftener. 'T is clownish to insist on doing all with one's own hands, as if every man should build his own clumsy house, forge his hammer, and bake his dough; but he is to dare to do what he can do best; not help others as they would direct him, but as he knows his helpful power to be. To do otherwise is to neutralize all those extraordinary special talents distributed among men. Yet whilst this self-truth is essential to the exhibition of the world and to the growth and glory of each mind, it is rare to find a man who believes his own thought or who speaks that which he was created to say. As nothing astonishes men so much as common sense and plain dealing, so nothing is more rare in any man than

---

38. Ippolito II d'Este (1509–1572), an Italian cardinal who took materials from Emperor Hadrian's (76–138) historic villa to furnish his own abode.

an act of his own. Any work looks wonderful to him, except that which he can do. We do not believe our own thought; we must serve somebody; we must quote somebody; we dote on the old and the distant; we are tickled by great names; we import the religion of other nations; we quote their opinions; we cite their laws. The gravest and learnedest courts in this country shudder to face a new question, and will wait months and years for a case to occur that can be tortured into a precedent, and thus throw on a bolder party the onus[39] of an initiative. Thus we do not carry a counsel in our breasts, or do not know it; and because we cannot shake off from our shoes this dust of Europe and Asia, the world seems to be born old, society is under a spell, every man is a borrower and a mimic, life is theatrical and literature a quotation; and hence that depression of spirits, that furrow of care, said to mark every American brow.

18 Self-trust is the first secret of success, the belief that if you are here the authorities of the universe put you here, and for cause, or with some task strictly appointed you in your constitution,[40] and so long as you work at that you are well and successful. It by no means consists in rushing prematurely to a showy feat that shall catch the eye and satisfy spectators. It is enough if you work in the right direction. So far from the performance being the real success, it is clear that the success was much earlier than that, namely, when all the feats that make our civility were the thoughts of good heads. The fame of each discovery rightly attaches to the mind that made the formula which contains all the details, and not to the manufacturers who now make their gain by it; although the mob uniformly cheers the publisher, and not the inventor. It is the dulness of the multitude that they cannot see the house in the ground-plan; the working, in the model of the projector. Whilst it is a thought, though it were a new fuel, or a new food, or the creation of

---

39. Rhymes with "bonus." Great responsibility.
40. Physical makeup.

agriculture, it is cried down, it is a chimera[41]; but when it is a fact, and comes in the shape of eight per cent., ten per cent., a hundred per cent., they cry, 'It is the voice of God.' Horatio Greenough[42] the sculptor said to me of Robert Fulton's[43] visit to Paris: "Fulton knocked at the door of Napoleon with steam, and was rejected; and Napoleon lived long enough to know that he had excluded a greater power than his own."

19 Is there no loving of knowledge, and of art, and of our design, for itself alone? Cannot we please ourselves with performing our work, or gaining truth and power, without being praised for it? I gain my point, I gain all points, if I can reach my companion with any statement which teaches him his own worth. The sum of wisdom is, that the time is never lost that is devoted to work. The good workman never says, 'There, that will do;' but, 'There, that is it: try it, and come again, it will last always.' If the artist, in whatever art, is well at work on his own design, it signifies little that he does not yet find orders or customers. I pronounce that young man happy who is content with having acquired the skill which he had aimed at, and waits willingly when the occasion of making it appreciated shall arrive, knowing well that it will not loiter. The time your rival spends in dressing up his work for effect, hastily, and for the market, you spend in study and experiments towards real knowledge and efficiency. He has thereby sold his picture or machine, or won the prize, or got the appointment; but you have raised yourself into a higher school of art, and a few years will show the advantage of the real master over the short popularity of the showman. I know it is a nice point to discriminate this self-trust, which is the pledge of all mental vigor and performance, from the disease

---

41. Pronounced kie-MEER-uh. (*Kie* rhymes with "pie.") Here, not the mythical monster but something unattainable, a silly dream.
42. Greenough (1805–1852), the sculptor commissioned to create a statue of George Washington for the centennial celebration of Washington's birth.
43. Fulton (1765–1815), an American engineer who invented the steamboat.

to which it is allied,—the exaggeration of the part which we can play;—yet they are two things. But it is sanity to know that, over my talent or knack, and a million times better than any talent, is the central intelligence which subordinates and uses all talents; and it is only as a door into this, that any talent or the knowledge it gives is of value. He only who comes into this central intelligence, in which no egotism or exaggeration can be, comes into self-possession.

20 My next point is that in the scale of powers it is not talent but sensibility which is best: talent confines, but the central life puts us in relation to all. How often it seems the chief good to be born with a cheerful temper and well adjusted to the tone of the human race. Such a man feels himself in harmony, and conscious by his receptivity of an infinite strength. Like Alfred, "good fortune accompanies him like a gift of God." Feel yourself, and be not daunted by things. 'T is the fulness of man that runs over into objects, and makes his Bibles and Shakspeares and Homers so great. The joyful reader borrows of his own ideas to fill their faulty outline, and knows not that he borrows and gives.

21 There is something of poverty in our criticism. We assume that there are few great men, all the rest are little; that there is but one Homer, but one Shakspeare, one Newton, one Socrates. But the soul in her beaming hour does not acknowledge these usurpations[44]. We should know how to praise Socrates, or Plato, or Saint John,[45] without impoverishing us. In good hours we do not find Shakspeare or Homer over-great, only to have been translators of the happy present, and every man and woman divine possibilities. 'T is the good reader that makes the good book; a good head cannot read amiss, in every book he finds passages which seem confidences or asides hidden from all else and unmistakably meant for his ear.

---

44. Pronounced yoo-ser-PAY-shunz. Usually applied to a position (like kingship); to "usurp" something is to take it from someone else unrightfully.
45. One of Jesus' twelve disciples.

22   The light by which we see in this world comes out from the soul of the observer. Wherever any noble sentiment dwelt, it made the faces and houses around to shine. Nay, the powers of this busy brain are miraculous and illimitable[46]. Therein are the rules and formulas by which the whole empire of matter is worked. There is no prosperity, trade, art, city, or great material wealth of any kind, but if you trace it home, you will find it rooted in a thought of some individual man.

23   Is all life a surface affair? 'T is curious, but our difference of wit appears to be only a difference of impressionability, or power to appreciate faint, fainter and infinitely faintest voices and visions. When the scholar or the writer has pumped his brain for thoughts and verses, and then comes abroad into Nature, has he never found that there is a better poetry hinted in a boy's whistle of a tune, or in the piping of a sparrow, than in all his literary results? We call it health. What is so admirable as the health of youth?—with his long days because his eyes are good, and brisk circulations keep him warm in cold rooms, and he loves books that speak to the imagination; and he can read Plato, covered to his chin with a cloak in a cold upper chamber, though he should associate the *Dialogues*[47] ever after with a woollen smell. 'T is the bane of life that natural effects are continually crowded out, and artificial arrangements substituted. We remember when in early youth the earth spoke and the heavens glowed; when an evening, any evening, grim and wintry, sleet and snow, was enough for us; the houses were in the air. Now it costs a rare combination of clouds and lights to overcome the common and mean. What is it we look for in the landscape, in sunsets and sunrises, in the sea and the firmament[48]? what but a compensation for the

---

46. Unable to be limited.
47. *Dialogues* is Plato's record of his mentor Socrates' conversations with various people. *Dialogues* captures Socrates' classic style of teaching by asking insightful questions.
48. Pronounced FER-muh-ment. The sky.

cramp and pettiness of human performances? We bask in the day, and the mind finds somewhat as great as itself. In Nature all is large massive repose. Remember what befalls a city boy who goes for the first time into the October woods. He is suddenly initiated into a pomp and glory that brings to pass for him the dreams of romance. He is the king he dreamed he was; he walks through tents of gold, through bowers of crimson, porphyry[49] and topaz, pavilion on pavilion, garlanded with vines, flowers and sunbeams, with incense and music, with so many hints to his astonished senses; the leaves twinkle and pique and flatter him, and his eye and step are tempted on by what hazy distances to happier solitudes. All this happiness he owes only to his finer perception. The owner of the wood-lot finds only a number of discolored trees, and says, 'They ought to come down; they are n't growing any better; they should be cut and corded before spring.'

24

Wordsworth[50] writes of the delights of the boy in Nature:—

> "For never will come back the hour
> Of splendor in the grass, of glory in the flower."[51]

25

But I have just seen a man, well knowing what he spoke of, who told me that the verse was not true for him; that his eyes opened as he grew older, and that every spring was more beautiful to him than the last.

26

We live among gods of our own creation. Does that deep-toned bell, which has shortened many a night of ill nerves, render to you nothing but acoustic vibrations? Is the old church which gave you the first lessons of religious life, or the village school, or the college where you first knew the dreams of fancy and joys of thought, only boards or brick and mortar? Is the house in which you were born, or the house in which your

---

49. Pronounced POR-fuh-ree. A crystal-like rock.
50. William Wordsworth (1770–1850), an English poet who often wrote about nature.
51. From "Intimations of Immortality from Recollections of Early Childhood."

dearest friend lived, only a piece of real estate whose value is covered by the Hartford insurance? You walk on the beach and enjoy the animation of the picture. Scoop up a little water in the hollow of your palm, take up a handful of shore sand; well, these are the elements. What is the beach but acres of sand? what is the ocean but cubic miles of water? a little more or less signifies nothing. No, it is that this brute matter is part of somewhat not brute. It is that the sand floor is held by spheral gravity, and bent to be a part of the round globe, under the optical sky,—part of the astonishing astronomy, and existing at last to moral ends and from moral causes.

27 The world is not made up to the eye of figures, that is, only half; it is also made of color. How that element washes the universe with its enchanting waves! The sculptor had ended his work, and behold a new world of dream-like glory. 'T is the last stroke of Nature; beyond color she cannot go. In like manner, life is made up, not of knowledge only, but of love also. If thought is form, sentiment is color. It clothes the skeleton world with space, variety and glow. The hues of sunset make life great; so the affections make some little web of cottage and fireside populous, important, and filling the main space in our history.

28 The fundamental fact in our metaphysic constitution is the correspondence of man to the world, so that every change in that writes a record in the mind. The mind yields sympathetically to the tendencies or law which stream through things and make the order of Nature; and in the perfection of this correspondence or expressiveness, the health and force of man consist. If we follow this hint into our intellectual education, we shall find that it is not propositions, not new dogmas and a logical exposition of the world that are our first need; but to watch and tenderly cherish the intellectual and moral sensibilities, those fountains of right thought, and woo them to stay and make their home with us. Whilst they abide with us we shall not think amiss. Our perception far outruns our talent. We bring a welcome to the highest lessons of religion and of poetry out of all proportion beyond our skill to teach. And, further, the great hearing and sympathy of men is more true and wise than their speaking is wont to be. A deep sympathy is what we require for any student of the mind; for the chief difference between man and man is a difference of impressionability. Aristotle or Bacon or Kant[52] propound some maxim which is the key-note[53] of philosophy thenceforward. But I am more interested to know that when at last they have hurled out their grand word, it is only some familiar experience of every man in the street. If it be not, it will never be heard of again.

29 Ah! if one could keep this sensibility, and live in the happy sufficing present, and find the day and its cheap means contenting, which only ask receptivity in you, and no strained exertion and cankering[54] ambition, overstimulating to be at the head of your class and the head of society, and to have distinction and laurels and consumption! We are not strong by our power to penetrate, but by our relatedness. The world is enlarged for us, not by new objects, but by finding more affinities and potencies in those we have.

30 This sensibility appears in the homage to beauty which exalts the faculties of youth; in the power which form and color exert upon the soul; when we see eyes that are a compliment to the human race, features that explain the Phidian sculpture. Fontenelle[55] said: "There are three things about which I have curiosity, though I know nothing of them,—music, poetry and love." The great doctors of this science are the greatest men,— Dante, Petrarch, Michel Angelo and Shakspeare. The wise

---

52. Immanuel Kant (1724–1804), a German philosopher who founded "transcendental idealism," a philosophy that says humans cannot know what reality is, only what it seems.
53. Main pillar.
54. Pronounced KAYNK-er-eeng. Here, corrupting or consuming.
55. Bernard Le Bovier de Fontenelle (1657–1757), a French author who wrote on scientific topics in a way that ordinary people could more easily understand.

Socrates treats this matter with a certain archness, yet with very marked expressions. "I am always," he says, "asserting that I happen to know, I may say, nothing but a mere trifle relating to matters of love; yet in that kind of learning I lay claim to being more skilled than any one man of the past or present time." They may well speak in this uncertain manner of their knowledge, and in this confident manner of their will, for the secret of it is hard to detect, so deep it is; and yet genius is measured by its skill in this science.

31   Who is he in youth or in maturity or even in old age, who does not like to hear of those sensibilities which turn curled heads round at church, and send wonderful eye-beams[56] across assemblies, from one to one, never missing in the thickest crowd? The keen statist reckons by tens and hundreds; the genial man is interested in every slipper that comes into the assembly. The passion, alike everywhere, creeps under the snows of Scandinavia, under the fires of the equator, and swims in the seas of Polynesia. Lofn[57] is as puissant[58] a divinity in the Norse Edda[59] as Camadeva[60] in the red vault of India, Eros[61] in the Greek, or Cupid[62] in the Latin heaven. And what is specially true of love is that it is a state of extreme impressionability; the lover has more senses and finer senses than others; his eye and ear are telegraphs; he reads omens on the flower, and cloud, and face, and form, and gesture, and reads them aright. In his surprise at the sudden and entire understanding that is between him and the beloved person, it occurs to him that they might somehow meet independently of time and place. How delicious the belief that he could elude all guards, precautions, ceremonies, means

---

56. Shining stares.
57. The Norse goddess of gentlenesss and sometimes forbidden love.
58. Pronounced PWIHS-nt. Powerful.
59. Two medieval Icelandic books: the *Prose Edda* and the *Poetic Edda*.
60. The Hindu god of romantic love.
61. The Greek god of romantic love.
62. The Latin version of Eros.

and delays, and hold instant and sempiternal[63] communication! In solitude, in banishment, the hope returned, and the experiment was eagerly tried. The supernal[64] powers seem to take his part. What was on his lips to say is uttered by his friend. When he went abroad, he met, by wonderful casualties, the one person he sought. If in his walk he chanced to look back, his friend was walking behind him. And it has happened that the artist has often drawn in his pictures the face of the future wife whom he had not yet seen.

32 But also in complacencies nowise so strict as this of the passion, the man of sensibility counts it a delight only to hear a child's voice fully addressed to him, or to see the beautiful manners of the youth of either sex. When the event is past and remote, how insignificant the greatest compared with the piquancy of the present! To-day at the school examination the professor interrogates Sylvina in the history class about Odoacer[65] and Alaric[66]. Sylvina can't remember, but suggests that Odoacer was defeated; and the professor tartly replies, "No, he defeated the Romans." But 't is plain to the visitor that 't is of no importance at all about Odoacer and 't is a great deal of importance about Sylvina, and if she says he was defeated, why he had better a great deal have been defeated than give her a moment's annoy. Odoacer, if there was a particle of the gentleman in him, would have said, Let me be defeated a thousand times.

33 And as our tenderness for youth and beauty gives a new and just importance to their fresh and manifold claims, so the like sensibility gives welcome to all excellence, has eyes and hospitality for merit in corners. An Englishman[67] of marked character

---

63. Pronounced sehm-puh-TERN-uhl. Eternal.
64. Pronounced suh-PERN-uhl. Heavenly.
65. Odoacer (433–493), a barbarian king of Italy.
66. Alaric (370–410), king of the Visigoths.
67. Charles Lane (1800–1870), an English transcendentalist who moved to America to try living a simple and commerce-free life. He founded a community (called Fruitlands) of like-minded people in Massachusetts, but it did not last.

and talent, who had brought with him hither one or two friends and a library of mystics, assured me that nobody and nothing of possible interest was left in England,—he had brought all that was alive away. I was forced to reply: "No, next door to you probably, on the other side of the partition in the same house, was a greater man than any you had seen." Every man has a history worth knowing, if he could tell it, or if we could draw it from him. Character and wit have their own magnetism. Send a deep man into any town, and he will find another deep man there, unknown hitherto to his neighbors. That is the great happiness of life,—to add to our high acquaintances. The very law of averages might have assured you that there will be in every hundred heads, say ten or five good heads. Morals are generated as the atmosphere is. 'T is a secret, the genesis of either; but the springs of justice and courage do not fail any more than salt or sulphur springs.

34 The world is always opulent, the oracles are never silent; but the receiver must by a happy temperance be brought to that top of condition, that frolic[68] health, that he can easily take and give these fine communications. Health is the condition of wisdom, and the sign is cheerfulness,—an open and noble temper. There was never poet who had not the heart in the right place. The old trouveur,[69] Pons Capdueil, wrote,—

35
"Oft have I heard, and deem the witness true,
Whom man delights in, God delights in too."

36 All beauty warms the heart, is a sign of health, prosperity and the favor of God. Everything lasting and fit for men the Divine Power has marked with this stamp. What delights, what emancipates, not what scars and pains us, is wise and good in speech and in the arts. For, truly, the heart at the centre of the

---

68. Pronounced FRAH-lihk. Jolly.
69. The trouveurs (pronounced troo-VEHRz) were medieval French epic poets who flourished during the eleventh through fourteenth centuries.

universe with every throb hurls the flood of happiness into every artery, vein and veinlet, so that the whole system is inundated with the tides of joy. The plenty of the poorest place is too great: the harvest cannot be gathered. Every sound ends in music. The edge of every surface is tinged with prismatic rays.

One more trait of true success. The good mind chooses what is positive, what is advancing,—embraces the affirmative. Our system is one of poverty. 'T is presumed, as I said, there is but one Shakspeare, one Homer, one Jesus,—not that all are or shall be inspired. But we must begin by affirming. Truth and goodness subsist[70] forevermore. It is true there is evil and good, night and day: but these are not equal. The day is great and final. The night is for the day, but the day is not for the night. What is this immortal demand for more, which belongs to our constitution? this enormous ideal? There is no such critic and beggar as this terrible Soul. No historical person begins to content us. We know the satisfactoriness of justice, the sufficiency of truth. We know the answer that leaves nothing to ask. We know the Spirit by its victorious tone. The searching tests to apply to every new pretender are amount and quality,—what does he add? and what is the state of mind he leaves me in? Your theory is unimportant; but what new stock you can add to humanity, or how high you can carry life? A man is a man only as he makes life and nature happier to us.

I fear the popular notion of success stands in direct opposition in all points to the real and wholesome success. One adores public opinion, the other private opinion; one fame, the other desert; one feats, the other humility; one lucre,[71] the other love; one monopoly, and the other hospitality of mind.

We may apply this affirmative law to letters, to manners, to art, to the decorations of our houses, etc. I do not find executions

---

70. Are sustained.
71. Pronounced LOO-ker. Money, as in the word "lucrative," with a negative connotation; ill-gotten gains.

or tortures or lazar-houses,[72] or grisly photographs of the field on the day after the battle, fit subjects for cabinet pictures. I think that some so-called "sacred subjects" must be treated with more genius than I have seen in the masters of Italian or Spanish art to be right pictures for houses and churches. Nature does not invite such exhibition. Nature lays the ground-plan of each creature accurately, sternly fit for all his functions; then veils it scrupulously. See how carefully she covers up the skeleton. The eye shall not see it; the sun shall not shine on it. She weaves her tissues and integuments[73] of flesh and skin and hair and beautiful colors of the day over it, and forces death down underground, and makes haste to cover it up with leaves and vines, and wipes carefully out every trace by new creation. Who and what are you that would lay the ghastly anatomy bare?

40

Don't hang a dismal picture on the wall, and do not daub[74] with sables[75] and glooms in your conversation. Don't be a cynic and disconsolate[76] preacher. Don't bewail and bemoan. Omit the negative propositions. Nerve us with incessant affirmatives. Don't waste yourself in rejection, nor bark against the bad, but chant the beauty of the good. When that is spoken which has a right to be spoken, the chatter and the criticism will stop. Set down nothing that will not help somebody;—

41

"For every gift of noble origin
Is breathed upon by Hope's perpetual breath."[77]

42

The affirmative of affirmatives is love. As much love, so much perception. As caloric[78] to matter, so is love to mind; so

---

72. Houses where people are quarantined.
73. Pronounced ihn-TEHG-yuh-muhnts. Enveloping layers.
74. Pronounced DAHB. Paint.
75. Pronounced SAY-buhlz. Mournful colors, usually black.
76. Pronounced dihs-KAHN-suh-lut. Mournfully dissatisfied.
77. From "October, 1803" in *Poems dedicated to National Independence* by Wordsworth.
78. Heat.

it enlarges, and so it empowers it. Good will makes insight, as one finds his way to the sea by embarking on a river. I have seen scores of people who can silence me, but I seek one who shall make me forget or overcome the frigidities and imbecilities[79] into which I fall. The painter Giotto, Vasari[80] tells us, renewed art because he put more goodness into his heads. To awake in man and to raise the sense of worth, to educate his feeling and judgment so that he shall scorn himself for a bad action, that is the only aim.

43

'T is cheap and easy to destroy. There is not a joyful boy or an innocent girl buoyant with fine purposes of duty, in all the street full of eager and rosy faces, but a cynic can chill and dishearten with a single word. Despondency[81] comes readily enough to the most sanguine[82]. The cynic has only to follow their hint with his bitter confirmation, and they check that eager courageous pace and go home with heavier step and premature age. They will themselves quickly enough give the hint he wants to the cold wretch. Which of them has not failed to please where they most wished it? or blundered where they were most ambitious of success? or found themselves awkward or tedious or incapable of study, thought or heroism, and only hoped by good sense and fidelity to do what they could and pass unblamed? And this witty malefactor[83] makes their little hope less with satire and skepticism, and slackens the springs of endeavor. Yes, this is easy; but to help the young soul, add energy, inspire hope and blow the coals into a useful flame; to

---

79. Pronounced ihm-buh-SIHL-uh-teez. Stupidities.
80. Georgio Vasari (1511–1574), an Italian painter, architect, and author who wrote the art history book *Lives of the Most Excellent Painters, Sculptors, and Architects* (1550).
81. Pronounced d'SPAHN-dehn-see. Sadness, dejectedness.
82. Pronounced SANG-wihn. Cheerful, bubbly.
83. Pronounced MAL-uh-fak-ter. The opposite of a benefactor, a malefactor is someone who means ill or works against you.

redeem defeat by new thought, by firm action, that is not easy, that is the work of divine men.

44 We live on different planes or platforms. There is an external life, which is educated at school, taught to read, write, cipher and trade; taught to grasp all the boy can get, urging him to put himself forward, to make himself useful and agreeable in the world, to ride, run, argue and contend, unfold his talents, shine, conquer and possess.

45 But the inner life sits at home, and does not learn to do things, nor value these feats at all. 'T is a quiet, wise perception. It loves truth, because it is itself real; it loves right, it knows nothing else; but it makes no progress; was as wise in our first memory of it as now; is just the same now in maturity and hereafter in age, it was in youth. We have grown to manhood and womanhood; we have powers, connection, children, reputations, professions: this makes no account of them all. It lives in the great present; it makes the present great. This tranquil, well-founded, wide-seeing soul is no express-rider, no attorney, no magistrate: it lies in the sun and broods on the world. A person of this temper once said to a man of much activity, "I will pardon you that you do so much, and you me that I do nothing." And Euripides[84] says that "Zeus hates busybodies and those who do too much."

---

84. Euripides (480–406 BC), a Greek playwright famous for tragedies.